Christ's Way to Pray

Books by Philip G. Samaan

Christ's Way of Reaching People
Christ's Way to Spiritual Growth
Christ's Way of Making Disciples
Blood Brothers
Portraits of the Messiah

To order, call **1-800-765-6955**.

Christ's Way to Pray

PHILIP G. SAMAAN

Author of *Christ's Way to Spiritual Growth*, *Christ's Way of Reaching People*, and *Christ's Way of Making Disciples*

The author assumes full responsibility for the accuracy of all facts and quotations as cited in this book.

Cover designed by EstiDzyn
Cover illustration by PhotoDisc
Typeset: 12/15 Bembo

PRINTED IN U.S.A.

07 06 05 04 03   5 4 3 2 1

ISBN 0-9741001-0-2

Printed by Review and Herald® Publishing Association

Dedication

Dedicated
to my beloved mother
whose passionate prayers were my first glimpse of
the embrace of the praying Jesus.

Contents

Introduction

Do your prayers seem to bounce off the wall and back into your face? Do you feel as if your petitions barely reach the ceiling before falling back shattered at your feet? Do your supplications seem like hollow and helpless echoes? How can our tainted prayers avail much when our righteousness is like filthy rags? How can our puny prayers become like those prevailing prayers we hear about?

Often we focus on the prayers of others in the Bible or in the church, hoping that their faith and fervency will rub off on us. While we gain much by studying the prayers of men and women like Jabez, Hannah, or Daniel, such prayers are not magical formulas for getting what we want. Prayer is not primarily about meeting our needs or promoting our prosperity; it is about deepening and enlarging our relationship with God. It is about widening *His* rule in our harried hearts and expanding *His* sovereignty in our sinful souls.

The prayer life of Jesus powerfully demonstrates His trusting and intimate relationship with His Father. Jesus' consuming passion was His Father's good pleasure, honor, and glory. Love and loyalty to His Father were His priorities. The domain of heaven was so enlarged in His heart that it knew no boundaries. How marvelous for Jesus to desire to engage us in His mighty prayer life! For in such a holy engagement His priority becomes our priority, and we experience God's all-encompassing reign in our hearts.

Knowing that we have faithful prayer warriors interceding for us and with us as we confront life's problems is encouraging. It buoys up our faith and confidence. But how much more encouraging it is to have Jesus as our faithful prayer warrior who ever lives to pray for us. How much more awesome to experience Christ as our prayer partner. For me, the experience of engaging my prayer life with that of Jesus' has been life-transforming. It has set me on a spiritual path with the praying Jesus, and helped me tap the inexhaustible resources of heaven. Our Mighty Petitioner is indeed "The Lord Our Righteousness" (Jer. 23:6), and His mighty prayers do avail much. My prayer life has never been the same since my puny and pitiful prayers became interconnected with His powerful and prevailing ones. Just as our righteousness is but filthy and tattered rags unless covered with His pure and perfect righteousness, so also our prayers are weak unless covered by His powerful prayers. Likewise, even our faith is feeble unless riveted in His mighty faith.

God wants to imbue our hearts with the unflinching courage that comes from knowing that Jesus perpetually prays for us. May the invincible confidence that comes from Christ's way of praying be ours. May we hear His vehement cries on our behalf, and may we see His shed tears as He prays passionately for us and with us. Jesus yearns to enfold us in this refuge of prayer. He longs to encircle us with His sympathizing human arm, and carry our prayers upon His mighty divine arm all the way to the throne. He desires to mingle the "much incense" of His perfect intercession and merits with our prayers. To take the sluggish trickle of our prayers and mingle it with the mighty flood of His prayers for us.

Are you ready to take the plunge? Let's go with the flow.

CHAPTER ONE

He Is Able

"Therefore He is also able to save to the uttermost those who come to God through Him" (Hebrews 7:25).

Striking up a pleasant conversation with my seatmate on a recent flight from Sacramento, I was startled to hear his assertion that Jesus could never save someone like him. When I inquired as to why he was so sure, he confided that he had been bearing a bitter grudge against his father since childhood. His heart had been full of hate toward him for more than 50 years. He remembered his drunken father beating and torturing his mother mercilessly before his eyes as he stood by helplessly. And then one day the father slashed his wife's throat while his son looked on. Amazingly, she survived this vicious assault. The son, however, became consumed with bitterness and hatred.

I asked him what had become of his father. "Ten years ago he put a gun to his head and killed himself," he blurted out. Yet this heavy load of hatred still poisoned and paralyzed the son's life. I explained to him that he had carried this crushing load for too long, that Jesus was longing to free him from this deadly bondage. Opening my pocket Bible, I read to him that Jesus is able to save to the *uttermost* those who come to Him. I told him that the word "uttermost" refers to complete deliverance for now and for all time. Jesus is capable of doing the impossible for us, the things that no one else can ever do.

As I explained how to release his long-held hatred over to Jesus, I found myself silently joining Jesus, the Mighty Petitioner, in praying for his deliverance. When he asked me to pray for him, I sensed as I prayed that Jesus was finally gaining the victory in this lifelong battle over his soul. He followed me in earnest prayer, giving over his hatred to Jesus, the Burden Bearer. The heavy fog of hatred finally lifted, and Christ's divine peace flashed across his face. God's amazing grace finally rescued him. His countenance was miraculously transformed. Unshackled, he kept repeating: "I'm free! Thank God I'm free! I'm finally free!"

HE CARES AND HE CAN

What an awesome and unique blessing we have in Jesus' ability to save to the uttermost. Often we do not pause to contemplate such an inestimable gift. It liberates us from the crushing burden of guilt. Releases us from the clutches of monstrous sins. Delivers us from a dreadful eternal death. Even the most skilled psychologist cannot do that. Billions of dollars for therapy would prove inadequate. The greatest power on earth is totally helpless to do anything for our souls. But the power of Christ is able to save us to the uttermost.

And why is He so infinitely able? Because Jesus lives for the purpose of praying for us. That is the solid basis for all that He does for us. He is not only a sympathetic friend but also an able intercessor. He cares and He can. With His gentle human arm He embraces us, and with His mighty divine arm He connects us with God's throne. Our friends may express some sympathy in the midst of our trials, but how many possess the ability to adequately deal with them? But, you see, we are Christ's project, and He is totally committed and capable to complete the project He started. Many of us can conceive of an idea but not follow through with it, or begin a project but never finish it. Isn't it quite refreshing to realize that Jesus stays the course to the end? He's not a quitter; He's a finisher.

HIS ABILITY, OUR AVAILABILITY

Whether Christ can start and finish His project depends on our response to Him. Do we let the Potter do His work on our clay? The secret for victory in our lives is continuously coming to Him, relinquishing self for the sake of seeking Him first. The greatest "good work" we can do before God is to continue coming to Jesus—no matter what. This is the easiest yet the most challenging work. Often this heart work—the uniting of our hearts with His heart—is the hardest work of all because it takes the total submission of self. But Jesus is always available and always able to help us. Availability and ability are His expertise.

So how then can we connect with His ability for us? By our availability to Him. Those who come to Him possess His solid promise that He will never cast them out (John 6:37). Thus we have absolutely no reason to shy away from coming to Him. This unshakable promise is combined with His invitation to go to Him with all our heavy burdens and exchange them for His peace that passes all understanding (Matt. 11:28).

This talk of Jesus' availability and ability takes my mind back to an unforgettable visit of a leprosarium in Africa.

Lepers were cast away by their relatives and left alone to suffer a slow and miserable death. Yet at that leprosarium, brave missionary nurses would defy the horrible sights of their oozing wounds, decaying flesh, and hideous disfiguration to minister to them every hour of every day. One morning after a few hours of visiting the place, I simply could not see anything more. I couldn't handle it; I had to stop and leave. I know that these devoted nurses could not have ministered so lovingly and patiently without the compassionate Jesus ministering through them. It is humanly impossible. "But with God all things are possible" (Matt. 19:26). There is absolutely no limit to what Christ can do through one person's availability to His ability. One who is available can truly say with Paul, "I can do all things through Christ who strengthens me" (Phil. 4:13).

In the leprosarium a thought pierced my mind: If these nurses were able to show such compassion for shunned lepers, how infinitely more is Jesus able to wrap His strong arms around me and to cleanse me of sin! If an earthly father engages in heroic feats to help his child, how exceedingly more is our all-loving and all-mighty Lord able to save to the uttermost those who come to Him. His valiant acts flow out of His big heart.

God's awesome ability is unleashed in response to our availability. When Jesus passes by, do we avail ourselves of His ability? The people of His hometown blocked His ability with their unavailability. He passed by Nazareth intending to work great deeds on their behalf, but He could not "because of their unbelief" (Matt. 13:58). Tragic, isn't it? They missed out on what Jesus had already planned to do simply because they would not avail themselves of His blessings. Could it be that Jesus had been passing by our Nazareths too, time and again? Has our unavailability been blocking His ability to do the great works He longs to do for us?

How often we scurry here, there, and everywhere—everywhere but to the presence of Christ. We desperately search for help from many experts before seeking the help of the Expert. He is able, all-loving, and wise. Why not tap into such a limitless resource? Why not see things from His perspective so that our lives may flow out of His gracious will? He longs to show Himself strong in our behalf when we place our full confidence in Him (2 Chron. 16:9). It greatly pleases Him to show off His amazing ability in response to our trusting availability.

HELP MY UNBELIEF

The unbelief of the people of Nazareth obstructed Christ's wondrous works among them. But don't we all have unbelief sometimes? Our faith falters and wanes. What sort of unbelief did the people of Nazareth have? According to the account, their unbelief resulted from their lack of appreciation of and trust in Jesus, possibly mixed with a good dose of arrogance and jealousy. No trust relationship with Jesus: that was the root of their problem.

Someone else confessed his unbelief to Jesus, but his heartfelt confession was born out of his distrust of self and trust in Christ. Remember the father who came to Jesus pleading for the healing of his tormented son? He burst into tears, throwing himself at His feet with the cry "Lord, I believe; help my unbelief!" (Mark 9:24). Yes, while we ponder our shaky faith and our struggle with unbelief, we need not despair. Let go of the bewilderment at Jesus' feet. Look away from yourself to the Savior. "Cast yourself at His feet with the cry 'Lord, I believe; help *Thou* mine unbelief.' You can *never* perish while you do this—*never*" (*The Desire of Ages,* p. 429; italics supplied).

Minutes earlier, the father had told Jesus that His disciples attempted to heal his tormented son, but they *"could not"* (verse 18). In this context, the father's urgent plea makes so much sense: "If You *can* do anything" (verse 22). In other words: "Your disciples could not. Can You?" It was a question of ability—their inability contrasted with His ability. And Jesus got down to the point when His disciples asked Him privately about their inability to heal the boy. "Why *could* we *not* cast it out?" they asked. Jesus answered: "This kind *can* come out by nothing but prayer and fasting" (verses 28, 29).

So to experience God's ability manifested in their lives, they should have made themselves available to Him through prayer and communion. Instead, they focused on their personal problems (*The Desire of Ages,* p. 431). Jesus Himself had just been transfigured, and even His ability resulted from His availability to His Father through prayer and communion. "He took Peter, John, and James and went up on the mountain to *pray*. As *He prayed,* the appearance of His face was altered" (Luke 9:28, 29).

JESUS IS ENOUGH

Recently I read a report about a frail mother who shifted a massive and crushing weight away from her child, saving him from certain death. If such a frail mother could accomplish such an incredible act because of love, how

18

much more our mighty and loving Jesus is able to save us to the uttermost! In His genius of mind and in His big heart, He has innumerable ways to accomplish heroic feats on our behalf. We see only our situation—a tiny sliver of our reality; but He looks at the whole spectrum of reality. His ability, manifested in our availability, is born out of His infinite love and wisdom. We may recount His miraculous ability in answering many of our prayers. Yet the greatest answered prayer is for Him to dwell in our lives and to become the center of our existence. When all is said and done, Jesus is enough. He is all we truly need.

I know a man who was severely beaten by thugs. He suffered head trauma, partial paralysis, and severe depression. He could not hold a job, lost many friends, and was on the verge of a nervous breakdown. He desperately sought human help, but soon discovered that it was inadequate. Even his devoted family could not help. He finally recognized that humanity—even at its best—could do only so much to help him. One dark day, when he was ready to end it all, he heard this encouraging voice piercing through his gloom: "You tried everything; why not try Jesus? When everything is said and done and you come to the end of your rope, you will finally discover that *Jesus is able, Jesus is enough."* In his despair these words about Jesus' ability and sufficiency seized him to the core. Burning in his mind as letters of fire, he kept repeating and believing them—Jesus is able, Jesus is enough—until his sanity returned and divine peace flooded his being.

Oh, let Jesus' ability and sufficiency seize my heart too. May my focus on Jesus turn me away from analyzing my own inability and inadequacy. This is the kind of divine help I really need. I can't still the raging storm and I can't calm the roaring sea. No, I can't; I am only human. But I know the One who can!

DISCUSSION QUESTIONS

1. What is the basis of Jesus' ability to save to the uttermost? How does His perpetual intercession play a part in this (Heb. 7:25)?

2. Jesus is both available and able. What does this mean to you?

3. Compare the relationship of Christ's ability and your availability. Why is it that we often focus on our own ability or inability? What difference does our focus make?

4. Contrast the unbelief of the people of Nazareth with the "unbelief" confessed by the father of the sick son.

5. Do you think that the father doubted Jesus' ability when he said, "If You can"? How does that relate to the disciples' inability to help him earlier? What attitude do you bring with you when you go to Jesus for help?

6. What are some things in your life that may block Jesus' ability to be manifested in you?

7. Think of a time in your spiritual journey when in your desperation and helplessness you finally recognized that Jesus was enough. What are some of the challenges that may hinder you from coming to the All-sufficient One? Do you now know the Man who can?

8. How would you pray this prayer in your own words: "Lord, I believe; help my unbelief"? Explain the apparent tension between belief and unbelief.

CHAPTER TWO

He Lives to Pray

"Therefore He is also able to save to the uttermost those who come to God through Him, since He always lives to make intercession for them" (Hebrews 7:25).

Mine was a praying mother. From my earliest days she impressed me as one who lived to pray. Until her last breath she never ceased to pray. Only that interrupted her fervent prayers. Prayer was her irrevocable commitment. It was the breath of her soul, her lifetime lifeline to God. Now my mother's breath is finally exhausted, but the Lord who had breathed into her His breath of life never ceases to pray for us. Just as Christ ever breathes life He ever breathes prayer. His prayers never cease, for He always lives to make intercession for us. He never forgets to pray or grows weary in praying, for He neither slumbers nor sleeps. What tremendous help and hope His mighty intercessions hold for us who live in the turmoil of this world!

INTERCESSION CONTINUUM

An acquaintance once confided to me that he felt it useless for him to intercede for the terminally ill. He felt defeated because he would pray and the sick ones would end up dying anyway. I learned later that he would pray only once or twice and then simply give up. No implicit trust in God's promises, no wrestling with God, no agonizing prayers or persistent knocking at the gates of heaven. Where are the prayer warriors whose hearts throb with the praying heart of Jesus? Those who live to pray as they breathe to live? Those who pray while embraced in the praying arms of Jesus?

Just as continuous breathing is indispensable to our existence, so is unceasing praying to our spiritual vitality. It is a continuum of inhaling God's love and life and exhaling our yearning for a deeper relationship with Him. This soul's vacuum for God becomes filled with such spiritual input and output. The apostle Paul correlates life with prayer when he asserts that Christ lives to make intercession (Heb. 7:25). Here is the surety of our salvation to the uttermost: His eternal life breathing forth His mighty intercessions.

So continuous salvation is interwoven with His continuous life of intercession. Jesus' continuum—to live, to pray, to save—is anchored in a duration of time that is eternal and a quality of salvation that is complete. But this does not mean that we can sit back and take it easy; it is rather a divine opportunity to unite ourselves actively with His intercessions. We are the special objects of Christ's intercession continuum, and through this we can "come to God through Him." It is there for us, for us to be swept up in its eternity and engulfed in its fullness. What prevents us from plunging into the eternal flow of such great intercession and salvation that issues forth from the heart of Jesus?

ALWAYS ON THE LINE

In our high-tech world we increasingly experience

more of the automated telephone answering system. Patiently waiting through countless impersonal commercials and service options, we finally may hear a live human voice that can offer real help. Yet our hope for help is quickly dashed when we find ourselves transferred in mid-sentence, only to start the automation process all over. Fortunately it is not always this impersonal. One time after waiting for what seemed like forever and being transferred to numerous wrong extensions, I appealed to the person on the line not to transfer me anywhere unless she let me complete my sentence so she would know what I really needed. The pleasant young woman on the line apologized for the merry-go-round and assured me that her job was to help frustrated customers like me. She was good to her word and took the time to give me the assistance I needed. What a relief! "Sir, is there anything else I can do to assist you?" she politely concluded.

This is what Jesus' ministry of intercession is about: taking all the time necessary to give real help. He has no automated system of communication, no answering machines. He doesn't play phone tag, hires no secretaries to say that He is not available, and retains no gatekeepers who make it difficult to have access to Him. He *Himself* is there on the line, full-time, giving real help. Every second, every minute, every hour, every day—He is always there to pray for us and with us, and to fit into His prayer life our particular concerns and needs. His life and His prayers are one. As surely as He lives, He prays. Jesus, our high priest, prays "according to the power of an endless life" (Heb. 7:16). This is His passion—His lifetime commitment. If we come to Him, He will never fail us.

MAGICAL FORMULA OR LIVING RELATIONSHIP?

What makes this kind of praying with Jesus a delight is the love relationship we enjoy with Him. It is not about an instant formula but an intimate relationship that permeates our daily lives. The perfunctory prayers we offer now and then do not reveal such intimate communion with Jesus. Imagine talking to our loving family members or trusted friends in such a haphazard manner. Yet often this is the sort of communication we have with Him. If we love and trust a person, then we feel at ease to be ourselves. We feel free to speak or to be quiet, to pray or to meditate, to recline or take a stroll. It is really the freedom to be, and the focus is not primarily on what we do but on the joy and security of being with a special person.

What an awesome privilege we have to commune freely with the God of all creation! To walk and talk daily with our friend Jesus! "It is a wonderful thing that we can pray effectually; that unworthy, erring mortals possess the power of offering their requests to God. What higher power can man desire than this—to be *linked with the infinite God?* Feeble, sinful man has the privilege of speaking to his Maker. We may utter words that reach the throne of the Monarch of the universe. We may speak with Jesus as we walk by the way, and He says, I am at thy right hand" (*Gospel Workers,* p. 258; italics supplied).

This is the sort of communion we need to have with Jesus. He desires to fill our lives with a heavenly atmosphere that imbues our daily activities and keeps our heart awake unto our Beloved. The most enjoyable visits I have with close friends are those in which we feel totally free to be ourselves without any pressure to occupy the time with any activity. In that trusting ambiance the right things just have a way of happening. "We may commune with God in our hearts; we may walk in companionship with Christ. When engaged in our daily labor, we may breathe out our heart's desire, inaudible to any human ear; but that word cannot die away into silence, nor can it be lost. Nothing can drown the soul's desire. It rises above the din of the street, above the noise of machinery" *(ibid.)*.

Isn't this what the apostle Paul is talking about when he tells us to "pray without ceasing" (1 Thess. 5:17)? Jesus said that "men always ought to pray and not lose heart" (Luke 18:1). Both are talking about prayer as a way of life. An atmosphere of trust that surrounds us, an environment of authentic heart-to-heart communion that envelops us. Such a spirit of prayer becomes interwoven into every facet of our lives just as the life-giving air we breathe. This is the kind of praying that is well described as "the breath of the soul," and "the secret of spiritual power" (*Gospel Workers,* p. 254). Breathing becomes indistinguishable from daily living unless we actually pause to think about it. As the breath of His life ever surges through every fiber of our being, so the breath of His Spirit immerses us in His mighty intercessions. He ever lives to pray for us and we ever live to pray with Him, and in the process our lives become transfigured into His likeness.

Prayer: Its Own Reward

Speaking of transfiguration, remember when Jesus took Peter, John, and James to witness Him praying on the mountain? Prayer was a way of life for Him, a normal part of His daily life. Notice that *as* He prayed, or as He was in the *process* of praying, He was transfigured (Luke 9:29). Communion with His Father transfigured Him to enjoy the mountaintop experience and to brave the valley of conflict. Our intimate fellowship in prayer with Jesus pervades our lives of prosperity as well as adversity. It becomes its own reward, for the greatest blessing in prayer is communion with Jesus. There is a rich blessing inherent in the very act of praying this way even when no petitions are evoked or denied, for the pleasure of His company is worth much more than anything else.

Such a transfigured prayer life anchored in His fellowship makes us minimize our petitions and maximize our praise of Him and the joy of His presence. He now has our undivided attention and free access to our heart. With peace and confidence we rest in His loving arms, knowing that He loves us, enjoys our company, and always wants the best for us. In His loving embrace we lack absolutely no good thing. Like a flower that welcomes the morning sun, with confidence we open our lives to Him at the breaking of every day, believing that He will work out His perfect will for us.

THE SUPERNATURAL OVERWHELMS THE NATURAL

Christ's intercession for us is constant and continuous. We may forget this reality, but He does not. We may become weary in praying, but He "shall neither slumber nor sleep" (Ps. 120:4). Like the mighty and unceasing flow of the Amazon River, so is His intercession for us. As the mighty Amazon has been flowing from time immemorial and will continue to flow until the end of time, so are the prayers of Jesus for us. Plunge into the flow of His life of prayer and feel the force of its current carry you along. Then, our focus cannot be on the trickle of our prayers' limitations but on the limitless and engulfing torrents of His prayers. The natural becomes overwhelmed with the supernatural and is rendered unconquerable.

It is Jesus' full-time ministry of intercession that counteracts Satan's full-time activity of accusation. Christ neither slumbers nor sleeps in His intercessions for us in order to thwart Satan's continuous accusations of us. Satan is "the accuser of our brethren, who accused them before our God day and night" (Rev. 12:10). This is a life-and-death struggle for people's souls and destinies. Therefore, with what flow do we go? With Satan's accusation or with Christ's intercession?

One of my students, battling incurable cancer, experienced the irresistible force of this divine flow of intercession. At first her desire and primary concern was that she would experience physical healing. But later this changed into buoyant confidence in Christ's salvation. She testified that He already had answered her greatest prayer request— regardless of what happened with her cancer. Before cancer she had been a lost soul, but through cancer she joyfully experienced salvation in Christ. The real miracle, she testified, was her conversion, abundant life, assurance of salvation, and the perfection of eternal life awaiting her. Merely being healed of cancer would be nothing in comparison to what she was now experiencing. She knew that the cancer attack was what had shocked her into evaluating her life choices and straightening out her priorities. Abundant life now was a precursor to the eternal life at Jesus' coming. That was her confidence and joy.

Isn't it amazing how often God's blessings lead us away from Him and afflictions draw us back to Him? We must live for the Savior and not the self, the Blesser and not the blessing. Jesus, in His ardent desire to save us to the uttermost, ever lives to pray for us. Let us ever live for Him.

DISCUSSION QUESTIONS

1. Take a moment to think about a friend or a relative who faithfully and consistently prayed for you, rain or shine. What spiritual impact did this have on your life?

2. How do you understand prayer as the breath of the soul? What do you think of this? Just as breath is indispensable to our physical existence, so is unceasing prayer; it is nothing contrived or forced, but something genuine and spontaneous.

3. What does Paul mean by exhorting us to pray without ceasing? To what extent have you experienced this? How does this relate to living our lives in the presence of God?

4. Compare your salvation to the uttermost in Christ with His life of intercession for you. How does knowing that Christ covers you with His all-embracing prayers make you feel?

5. Think of a frustrating time when you tried to reach someone on the phone, but to no avail. You were lost in the maze of phone tag, voice mail, recorded messages, being put on hold or transferred. Compare this to our Lord, who is always live on the line.

6. When you visit with friends, do you feel that you need to keep the conversation going? Does silence bother

you or them? How does this apply to your communion with Christ?

7. What does it take for our petitions to evolve more and more into praise? Explain.

8. Consider this statement from Ellen White in view of Christ's priority of praying for you: "Letters come to me in which the writers ask me to pray for them. But Christ is praying for them. All they need is to carry their soul-distress to Jesus" (*Sermons and Talks*, vol.2, p.148)

CHAPTER THREE

He Prays Passionately

"Who, in the days of His flesh, when He had offered up prayers and supplications, with vehement cries and tears" (Hebrews 5:7).

My mother not only lived to pray, she prayed *passionately* for me. Often when I would hear her cries and see the tears mingled with her prayers to God, I would be struck by a holy intensity written all over her face. She seemed to be in the presence of God, pouring out her heart to Him as to her best friend. I was impressed by such passionate praying, but would wonder what it was all about. Later on I learned that her cries and tears were poured out for me, her son. I left home as a teenager, never to return. But I was always told that she prayed for me unceasingly until her death a few decades later. Even her last breaths whispered a fervent prayer. She indeed lived to pray and to pray passionately—a tiny glimpse of how Jesus prays for me.

TRANSFORMING PRAYER

Needless to say, such persistent and passionate praying of my mother impacted my entire life. But if such prayers of my mother so affected my life, how exceedingly more the passionate prayers of Jesus! Once I was told a legend about a loving and praying mother who sacrificed all for her little boy. In his adolescence he joined a gang and lived a life of crime and violence. Yet his devoted mother never forgot to love him and pray for him. One night he entered his mother's house, drunk with alcohol and violence and determined to obey the orders of his heartless gang members to bring back his mother's heart. In a fit of anger he cut out her heart as she pleaded with him. Running back to his waiting gang, he stumbled and fell, dropping his mother's heart on the hard ground. Her heart cried out, "Son, be careful; don't hurt yourself. No matter what, I will always love you." His mother's broken heart broke his heart and transformed his life. What she could not accomplish in her life she accomplished through her death.

Praying With All Our Heart

For each one of us, Jesus, our loving intercessor, died of a broken heart. Imagine the heartrending scene on the cross. Breathing His last breath, Jesus looked with pity upon His killers and cried out in agony for them: "Father, forgive them, for they do not know what they do" (Luke 23:34). If He so fervently prayed for His enemies who inflicted a fatal stab to His heart, He certainly is willing to pray with such passion for us. His broken heart cries out not in vengeance, but in love and forgiveness.

In a culture that pursues pleasure and peddles hedonism it is difficult to express deep emotion in prayer. When was the last time we wept in contrition for wounding the heart of Jesus? What about a world that is lost in sin and doomed to destruction? Do we shed tears in prayer for it? Does our self-centered society keep our hearts hard and keep our eyes dry? Our hearts must be broken with the heart of Jesus for a broken world. But have you noticed that some people apologize and feel embarrassed when overcome by their tears? Remember that Jesus wept. And when we enter into His travail for the lost, we will weep as well.

This wise admonition of Solomon sounds strange and incongruous in our Western ears: "Better to go to the house of mourning than to go to the house of feasting," and "Sorrow is better than laughter, for by a sad countenance the heart is made better. The heart of the wise is in the house of mourning, but the heart of fools is in the house of mirth" (Eccl. 7:2-4). Solomon did not mean that to be morose or to entertain morbid thoughts was good. He spoke from his own personal experience, for He enjoyed life's pleasures to the fullest. However, He also knew well that sorrow often leads us to examine our lives and the destiny awaiting us. It is really a blessing in disguise, for mourning can center our priorities, soften our hearts, subdue and refine our characters. Paradoxically, such godly sorrow results in a joyful heart, whereas frivolous feasting and merrymaking can lead to inward sorrow.

A pastor who got teary-eyed once in a while when preaching was teased as the "weeping prophet." It turned many of his parishioners off, making his sermons less effective. Our society pressures us to put on a happy face no matter how tortured inside we are. One of my bright and popular students came to see me in my office. I was surprised when her mask of smiles dropped to reveal a sad face. She confided that she was really miserable inside but she dared not reveal that publicly. She felt she must keep up a cheerful facade and put on a brave front in order to remain popular with her friends. She did not say much else during that appointment; she just wanted to be in a safe place where she could feel free to be sad, to be herself without feeling rejected.

AND JESUS WEPT

Since Jesus is our model for healthy human expression, His example transcends any cultural background. He was a real man with real human emotions. Jesus wept over Jerusalem (Luke 19:41), and wailed about its desperate condition. "O Jerusalem, Jerusalem," He cried out. "How often I wanted to gather your children together, as a hen gathers her chicks under her wings, but you were not willing!" (Matt. 23:37). Jesus, the Son of man and our supreme example, did not shy away from expressing His emotion for the lost. What a compassionate Savior! His agonizing tears and lamenting voice flowed freely from His big heart.

Contemplate this stirring description of that scene in the book *The Desire of Ages*. The people "are surprised and disappointed to see His eyes fill with tears, and His body rock to and fro like a tree before the tempest, while a wail of anguish bursts from His quivering lips, as if from the depths of a broken heart." The angels in heaven were struck with amazement. "What a sight was this for angels to behold! their loved Commander in an agony of tears!" Also, "It was the sight of Jerusalem that pierced the heart of Jesus." For "Jerusalem had been the child of His care, and as a tender father mourns over a wayward son, so Jesus wept over the beloved city" (pp. 575-577).

"Jesus wept" is the shortest verse in the Bible (John 11:35) and reveals Jesus' sympathetic heart. His tears were shed in comradery with the grieving Mary, Martha, and their friends. But even more, His tears were spilled for the lost in the crowd and in the world. "The woes of the sinful race were heavy upon His soul, and the fountain of His tears was broken up as He longed to relieve all their distress" (*The Desire of Ages,* p. 534). The reference to Jesus weeping (verse 35) fits between the references to His groaning (verses 33, 38). Hence, shedding tears was preceded and followed by the strong emotional expression of groaning. His emotions were not only seen but heard. This seems to resonate with Christ's strong emotions in His prayer expressed in "vehement cries and tears" in our text of Hebrews 5:7. As it is evident in the context, Jesus' groaning and weeping culminated in His prayer to His Father for the raising of His dear friend Lazarus (John 11:41). In this one act Jesus painted a powerful picture of God's identification with His creatures' pain and suffering.

SWEAT AND BLOOD

These tears for the rejecters of His grace were a prologue to the tears He was to shed for wayward Jerusalem. And they were strongly reinforced by His passionate praying in the Garden and on the cross. It is evident that He prayed most intensely in the Garden of Gethsemane. *Gethsemane* comes from Aramaic, which literally means "oil press"—a fitting description for His soul being pressed unto death. I have often witnessed how an oil press functions in extracting oil from olives. The giant stone wheels roll over and crush the olives to pulp, releasing its precious oil. Likewise, Christ's life was crushed by the heavy weight of this sinful world, releasing His precious blood of salvation.

Here is Luke's compelling account: "And being in agony, He prayed more earnestly. And His sweat became like great drops of blood falling down to the ground" (22:44). "In agony," "prayed more earnestly," "sweat," and "blood." Matthew describes the same experience with these words: "sorrowful," "deeply distressed," "exceedingly sorrowful, even unto death," "fell on His face" (26:37-39). That was the stuff that made up Christ's passionate praying. "The humanity of the Son of God trembled in that trying hour," and "the fate of humanity trembled in the balance" (*The Desire of Ages,* p. 690).

"His sweat became like great drops of blood." The word "drops" comes from the Greek *thromboi,* which means "clots" or "thick drops," resulting from sweat mixed with blood. This unusual phenomenon is referred to as *diapedesis,* a Greek term that literally means "leaping through." Thus—blood leaping through sweat. It is a medical term depicting the sweat of blood. This condition results from a bursting of capillaries caused by violent excitement or sudden terror. Christ was suffering under this shuddering terror of a world condemned to eternal separation from God. That is why His soul was in such agony— even unto death. It was a life-and-death struggle for the fate of humanity. A struggle in which Satan was determined to terrorize and hijack Planet Earth to its utter destruction.

Right after this Jesus prayed three times for this cup to be taken away from Him. Yet He was totally submissive to His Father's will (Matt. 26:38-44). He felt revulsion at drinking the cup, but His heroic love for sinful humanity won the hour. He was persistent and passionate, for He prayed this prayer three times, crying out, "O My Father."

Here it is revealed that He was in deep distress and in desperate need for help in drinking the cup. And what does drinking the "cup" signify? It is nothing less than God's unmixed wrath against sin. An awful wrath not watered down to make it bearable, not mixed with mercy. This cup of unmixed wrath against sin was to be drunk by Jesus. "For He made Him who knew no sin to be sin for us, that we might become the righteousness of God in Him" (2 Cor. 5:21).

GOD WAS IN CHRIST

No hint whatsoever should be inferred here that the Father is less loving and merciful than His Son, or that He is more intent on exacting justice. In the face of Jesus we see the face of God. His heart was broken along with the heart of His Son as both suffered in Gethsemane and Golgotha. For "God was in Christ reconciling the world to Himself" (2 Cor. 5:19). Maybe the Father, in a way, suffered even more than His Son. Can you imagine the Father, with all the love and power at His command, having to watch His only beloved Son experience the worst suffering, torture, and death? I have an only daughter, and I suffer more than she when I see her suffer. I would do anything to trade places with her and take upon myself her suffering.

Therefore when Christ prayed passionately for Himself and for humanity, in no way was He trying to make Himself or us more lovable. The Father loves His Son. He loves us as much as He loves Him. And when Jesus prays for us, He desires for us to join the close fellowship He enjoys with the Father. He does not pray so that He may twist God's arm to finally go along with His desire, for both have the same desire. Considering the crucial issues of the great controversy, He desires humanity to cooperate with divinity in order that God's will may be fulfilled.

From a Thorn to the Throne

Paul must have seen a glimpse of the persistence and passion of Jesus praying with "vehement cries and tears" in the Garden. Nowhere is it more clear than in 2 Corinthians 12:7-10 when Paul himself "pleaded with the Lord three times that it [a thorn in the flesh] might depart from me" (verse 8). In Greek the word used for "thorn" is *skolpos,* meaning a sliver, splinter, or a small piece of wood. I believe that Paul's thorn was his weak eyesight. We each have our "cup" to drink; that was his "cup" to drink. His thorn in the flesh was to always remind him of his calling and the all-sufficiency of God's grace.

The apostle prayed passionately *three times* for the *thorn* to be removed, and Jesus vehemently prayed *three times* for the *cross* to be taken away from Him. Not a little sliver of wood but cruel thorns pierced His brow. Not a tiny splinter of wood but spikelike nails tore at His flesh. Not a *skolpos* of a puny piece of wood but two massive wooden beams of a rugged cross tormented Him. He was scarred for this life and for eternity. "My dear Paul whom I called on the way to Damascus," Jesus would say. "I know exactly how you feel. Why not let your tiny wooden sliver be buried in My huge wooden cross?" Jesus would continue: "My apostle Paul, why not let your three urgent pleas be immersed in My three passionate pleas; and let your will be submerged in My will, for My grace is all-sufficient. Paul, why not let your thorn in the flesh lead you to My throne in glory?"

TEACH US TO PRAY

Christ vividly exemplified passionate praying before His disciples. He drew them away from the thorns of their daily lives and pulled them up with Him to the throne of God's presence. When it came to His praying, one thing the disciples knew for sure was that it was vastly different than the formalized prayers to which they were accustomed. What was it about His kind of praying that made such an impact on them? They frequently saw Him caught up in intimate communion with His Father, seemingly unaware of His surroundings yet focused on interceding for them. "He prayed, often with strong crying and tears. He prayed for His disciples and for Himself, thus identifying Himself with human needs. He was a mighty petitioner. As the Prince of life, He had power with God, and prevailed" (*Gospel Workers,* p. 256).

On certain occasions He would pray all night. The disciples, retiring for the night, would wake up in the morning and find Him still praying. The intensity written on His face, the earnestness flowing through His voice, and the passionate pleas on His lips convinced them that He was surrounded by God's presence. We can to some degree understand how they felt hearing their Master pray. We hear a few people pray, and we know for certain that they are in touch with heaven. Some others we hear pray, and it seems that they are praying to themselves or others around them.

One day as Jesus was praying in this passionate way, they felt that this was the kind of prayer life they really needed. So one of them blurted out, "Lord, teach us to pray" (Luke 11:1). "Seeming unconscious of their presence, He continued praying aloud," Ellen White describes the poignant scene. "The Saviour's face was irradiated with a celestial brightness. He seemed to be in the presence of the Unseen, and there was a living power in His words as of one who spoke with God" (*Thoughts From the Mount of Blessing,* p. 102). Moreover, Jesus "supplicated the throne of God, till His humanity was charged with a heavenly current that connected humanity with divinity" (*Education,* pp. 80, 81).

The Lord's Prayer recorded in Luke 11:2-4 and also in Matthew 6:9-13 is to serve as a practical illustration, not in precision but in pattern. This whole prayer is distilled into Christ's desire to connect us as sons and daughters with the Father. His use of the phrase "Our Father" indicates that He wanted to share His intimate relationship with His Father with us. His heavenly kingdom was to rule in our fallen world, and His divine will was to become sovereign in our human hearts. This connection between heaven and earth leads us to act like our Father. To forgive others as we were forgiven, for example. Thus at the end, when Christ comes to share His kingdom with us, we will share also in His power and glory forever.

Once I heard a speaker sum up the Lord's Prayer in three words: give, forgive, and deliver. These constitute three progressive levels of importance in prayer:

1. **"Give** us this day our daily bread."
2. **"Forgive** us our debts, as we forgive our debtors."
3. **"Deliver** us from the evil one."

This prayer does not merely help us with our life on

this earth, but also connects us with His heavenly kingdom. "Your kingdom come. Your will be done on earth as it is in heaven" (Matt. 6:10). In His glorious kingdom we shall see Him face to face. There will be no more need to give, for we will inherit all things with Christ. No need to forgive, for all will be forgiven. No need to deliver from the evil one, for there will be no more evil. What a day that will be when we shall see Him in all His glory!

PASSION MERGED IN SUBMISSION

How is our prayer life today? Is it earnest and passionate? persistent and persevering? Do we sense ourselves enclosed in God's presence, communing with Him as with our best friend? Do we yearn to enlarge the territory of our heart so that our passion for Him may be merged with our submission to Him? As we follow His example, He wants our humanity to be charged with divinity. And as our Elder Brother in the family of God, He desires us to join Him in connecting with "our" Father in heaven—the same Father for Him and for us.

My mother's passionate praying for me was transferred into my own prayer life. As a child, I remember the miracle that took place as I earnestly prayed for her, as she was deathly sick. We lived out in the country and lacked any modern amenities. There was only one old car in the village. My father and his friend planned to use this car on a business trip to a faraway city. Soon after they left that morning, my mother became terribly ill. There was no way to contact anyone and no medical help available nearby. I felt totally helpless to do anything for my mother, she who had always helped me and prayed for me.

I was so worried that my only recourse became prayer. The mother who prayed so earnestly for me now needed my earnest prayer for her. As never before, I entered into a passionate season of intercessory prayer for her. I just could not let go of God until He blessed me with some indication that He was going to do something. I persisted in prayer with crying and tears until I got the assurance that help was on the way. An overwhelming conviction that God's will was for my father to come back and for my mother to get well seized me. My passionate praying to God seemed to become submerged in my total submission to Him.

I quietly and trustingly waited for something to happen. Later on that morning my father and his friend returned home wondering what the trouble was. Apparently while I had been praying, a strong conviction seized my father to abort the trip immediately and return home. The happy ending: He drove my mother to a physician and her life was spared just in time. I had prayed following her example. As my mother often prayed for me with all her heart, now I was praying for her with all my heart.

"When with earnestness and intensity we breathe a prayer in the name of Christ, there is in that very intensity a pledge from God that He is about to answer our prayer 'exceedingly abundantly above all that we ask or think'" (*Christ's Object Lessons,* p. 147).

Discussion Questions

1. Have you ever had a friend or a loved one who prayed for you passionately, wholeheartedly? Briefly describe such an experience and its implications for your life.

2. What does it tell you about the heart of Jesus that He pleaded, "Father, forgive them for they do not know"? What difference would it make if you prayed like this? Why?

3. Why is it hard for us to express our emotions? What kinds of emotions need to be expressed, and what kinds need to be dealt with? Why?

4. Have you ever experienced that mourning is better than feasting? How, in your life, do you apply Solomon's admonition that sorrow is better than laughter?

5. How does it make you feel to know that Jesus, the Son of God, expressed strong emotions in His prayers? And that He still prays this way for you? What room, if any, may such emotional expression have in your intercessory prayer? Would that make a difference?

6. Have you ever had what may be described as a "sweat and blood" experience in prayer? How would you describe such an experience? What healing, restoration resulted from it?

7. What "thorn in the flesh" have you been pleading with God about? How do you relate that to the cross of Christ? Has your thorn led you to the throne? Explain how.

CHAPTER FOUR

He Prays for Us

"And the Lord said, 'Simon, Simon! Indeed, Satan has asked for you, that he may sift you as wheat. But I have prayed for you, that your faith should not fail'" (Luke 22:31, 32).

One of my students came by my office needing me to pray for her. She explained that whenever her roommate prayed for her she felt spiritually strong. But now that her roommate had transferred to another university she felt no incentive to pray alone. She felt she was losing her hold on Jesus. Her friend's strong faith in praying for her buttressed her faith and boosted her courage. She felt much better after I prayed for her and assured her that Jesus had joined us in that prayer. I assured her that though her prayer partner had left, Jesus was still her mighty intercessor. Indeed, she would never have to pray alone—roommate or no roommate—because her powerful Prayer Warrior ever lives to pray for her.

PLUNGING INTO THE TORRENTS

I can relate to my student's experience. The earnest prayers of my prayer partners boost my faith, too, in times of need. Some time ago I was agonizing over a tough decision I had to make. I sought out a trustworthy friend, a man of prayer, to pray for me. As he earnestly prayed for me, God seemed so real and near. He prayed with such faith, power, and fervency that my heart was flooded with assurance that God was in control and that things were going to work out. It was quite evident that my good friend was in touch with God, and his sturdy faith bolstered my shaky faith and put me in touch with God.

Reflecting back on these two incidents, I was gripped with this awesome thought: If the prayers of faithful friends can make such a huge impact on our lives, how much more can the mighty prayers of Jesus! He is the perfect prayer partner, possessing infinite faith, who constantly and fervently prays for us. Touching a trickle of cool water can be refreshing, but how much better to plunge into the mighty torrents of a rushing river. What a tremendous difference it would make in our prayer life to live out this as a spiritual reality! His mighty prayers for us are effective and prevailing because they are imbued with His infinite love, wisdom, and power. He discerns our innermost thoughts and feelings, as He also discerns the infinite mind of God. What a rich and indispensable resource of effectual prayer we have in Jesus! Why not tap into this inexhaustible reservoir He has in reserve for us?

THE MIGHTY PRAYER WARRIOR

Exciting events took place when Jesus prayed for others. And Jesus' prayers changed not only the situation but the lives of those involved. Jesus prayed for others, and He even prayed for Himself. His prayers were anchored in unbroken communion with His Father. Early mornings and late nights found Him engaged in prayer (Mark 1:35; Luke 5:16; 6:12). At His baptism He raised His gaze to heaven, pouring out a prayer before the formidable challenge awaiting Him in His ministry (Luke 3:21). In the garden, from His broken heart flowed a passionate prayer of sweat and blood, a plea to His Father (Matt. 26:36-44).

John 17 records by far the most extensive intercessory prayer of Jesus. Jesus first prayed for Himself (verses 1-5), then for His disciples (verses 6-19), and finally for all other believers (verses 20-26). He intercedes for specific people and priorities. The thrust of this mighty prayer is Christ's ardent desire for His disciples and all believers to share what He enjoys with the Father: the unity, mutual love and trust, faithfulness, truth, unity, joy, consecration, and mission. Without a doubt this prayer of intercession was— and continues to be—effectual in the lives of believers. And not only that, every time Christ's faithful followers unite themselves with Him in this prayer, His petitions will be fulfilled in their lives.

At times we may excuse ourselves from uniting with Christ in prayer because of our busy schedules. But if we say that we have no time to pray, then in effect we are saying we have no time to live. Since prayer is the breath of the soul, such excuses make no sense. How ridiculous it would be to see a man suffocating for lack of air while protesting that he has no time to breathe. But how often is this the case in our spiritual lives? Wasn't Jesus' life busy? Yet He constantly made prayer a top priority. It was the breath of His soul as well, the living connection with the source of power that made His perilous mission possible. "No other life was ever so crowded with labor and re- sponsibility as was that of Jesus; yet how often He was found in prayer! How constant was His communion with God!" (*The Desire of Ages,* p. 362).

"I HAVE PRAYED FOR YOU!"

Anchored in intimate communion with His Father, Jesus' fervent prayers for others were prevailing. Peter was one disciple for whom Jesus prayed. Peter had been in His prayers for a while because He knew that Satan was after him. "Simon, Simon! Indeed, Satan has asked for you, that he may sift you as wheat" (Luke 22:31). At the beginning of Christ's ministry, when He called this disciple to follow Him (John 1:42), He changed his name from Simon to Cephas (Peter). So why was He now calling Peter by his old name—Simon—and why was He using it twice? Probably because the name "Simon" in Hebrew refers to hearing. And Jesus wanted Peter to be alert and attentive to what He was about to tell him. What crucial warning did Jesus have for His disciple? A warning about the adversary. Satan was doggedly pursuing him. He desired to have him and to destroy his faith as Christ's ministry was coming to an end. This is the focused mission of Satan: Seek and destroy the faith of Christ's followers.

Often we stop with verse 31 and do not proceed to the next verse of this human-supernatural encounter. We focus on Satan's attacks instead of joining in Christ's mighty prayers for us. We see Satan lurking around every corner and hiding behind every bush. And Satan delights to have all the attention he can get! Therefore what Satan does must never be viewed in isolation from what Christ does. Let Satan desire to have us as much as he wants to. Christ desires to have us infinitely more. His desire eclipses Satan's, rendering it null and void. Verse 32 begins with a rebuttal to the enemy, with what I call the "divine but." *"But* I have prayed for you, that your faith should not fail."

Jesus alerts Peter to his pending peril, but He does not leave him there. Immediately Jesus points him to His powerful prayer for him.

Yet in spite of Jesus' prevailing prayer for Peter—that his faith should not fail—his faith did fail when he denied his Master three times. Even Christ Himself would not impose His will on Peter; Peter had to choose freely to avail himself of such intercessory prayer. This clearly shows the indispensable need for Peter to cooperate with Jesus' powerful prayers for him. He must humble himself in submission, placing his full trust in Him. His faith would not have failed if he had anchored his weak faith in the mighty faith of Jesus, and had placed himself in Jesus' domain. It was said of Daniel's and his companions' prayers that "in faith they prayed for wisdom, and they *lived their prayers*. They *placed* themselves where God *could bless* them" (*Prophets and Kings*, p. 486; italics supplied).

But shortly after, Peter learned the valuable lesson of humility when, with bitter tears of remorse, he wholeheartedly repented of his pride and self-sufficiency. He lived his sincere prayers of repentance. Even in this apparent failure, Christ gained the final victory in Peter's life. Such experience of sincere repentance not only solidified his commitment to Christ but also helped to strengthen the faith of many others. Let us never despair on account of our defeat, for in Christ our defeat can be transformed into decisive victory.

Imagine for a moment that you are in the midst of a terrible crisis. How would you feel if Jesus addressed you by name and told you that He was praying for you? If a faithful friend says to you that he is praying for you, you would feel strengthened and encouraged. But Jesus is no ordinary praying friend. He is called "Wonderful, Counselor, Mighty God, Everlasting Father, Prince of Peace" (Isa. 9:6), and He prays for us like He prayed for Peter. Satan can no longer find a foothold here, for he has to deal with Jesus Himself. "Satan trembles and flees before the *weakest soul* who finds refuge in that mighty name [of Jesus]" (*The Desire of Ages,* p. 131; italics supplied). If you truly believed that the Son of God Himself is praying for you, wouldn't it revolutionize your prayer life? Yet this is Christ's reality for you: He knows you by name, He is intimately acquainted with your problems, and He cares so much for you that He tailors His prayers to suit your particular needs.

When Jesus prays for us He "knows all about our burdens, our dangers, and our difficulties; and He fills His mouth with arguments in our behalf. *He fits His intercessions to the needs of each soul,* as He did in the case of Peter" Moreover, "With His upraised hands He pleads, 'I have graven thee upon the palms of my hands.' God loves to hear, and responds to the pleadings of His Son" (*The Seventh-day Adventist Bible Commentary,* Ellen G. White Comments, vol. 7, pp. 931, 948; italics supplied). Isn't it amazing that Jesus not only prays passionately for us but also adapts His mighty prayers to make them fit the specific needs and problems we face? What an act of condescension on His part: To take His perfect prayers and adjust them to our imperfect prayers and shortsighted human petitions!

PERFECT PRAYER FOR PERFECT PROBLEM

If we think Simon Peter had problems for Jesus to pray

for, imagine the almost hopeless situation of Mary Magdalene. She had seven colossal problems. Mary was possessed by not one demon but seven of them (Luke 8:2; Mark 16:9). With the number seven representing perfection, Mary had a huge problem. Yes, the devil was after Peter, but he was after Mary even more with his full hellish force. He desired to have Peter, but Mary was his possession seven times over.

In praying for Mary, Jesus could read the sealed pages of her heart, and fully understand her unfortunate circumstances. He could look beyond the sevenfold demon possession and discern her potential to become one of His most devoted followers. What a wonderful Savior we have who cuts through demonic hell and comes up with glorious hope. "It was He [Jesus] who had lifted her from despair and ruin. Seven times she had heard His rebuke of the demons that controlled her heart and mind. *She had heard His strong cries to the Father in her behalf* . . . and in His strength she had overcome" (*The Desire of Ages,* p. 568; italics supplied).

Imagine Mary hearing her name on Jesus' praying lips. She listened to His strong cries and realized that such a passionate outpouring of His heart to the Father was just for her. No wonder her life was forever transformed. And if Christ's mighty prayers prevailed in Peter's and Mary's lives, they certainly can prevail in your life and mine. However tightly seemingly insurmountable problems hedge us in, Jesus has a way of escape for us.

JESUS PRAYED FOR FRIENDS AND ENEMIES

Jesus often prayed for His disciples. It is recorded that

even before choosing them He "went out to the mountain to pray, and continued all night in prayer to God" (Luke 6:12). When was the last time you and I prayed all night for someone, or about some important decision? One wonders how Jesus filled the entire night with supplications to the Father for His disciples. During His ministry He would plead with God for each individual disciple, for his particular needs and challenges. He petitioned His Father for their faith not to fail, for His will to be done in their lives, and for their salvation and the salvation of many through them.

"For hours He continued pleading with God. Not for Himself but for men were those prayers. . . . In travail and conflict of soul He prayed for His disciples. . . . For them, the burden was heavy upon His heart, and He poured out His supplications with bitter agony and tears" (*The Desire of Ages,* p. 379). This selfless and passionate act of total devotion to them and their ministry reveals the praying heart of Jesus. They were in His heart, and we too are in His heart; and He is as willing and committed to pray for us now as He prayed for them then. After all, "Jesus Christ is the same yesterday, today, and forever" (Heb. 13:8).

Jesus prayed not only for His disciples but also for all others who would believe in Him (John 17:6-26). His earnest prayer was saturated with love for all. He prayed that they be one with Him and each other, and that they be with Him forever in glory. And on the cross His very first utterances were not at all about Himself or His disciples, but took the form of a pleading prayer for His bitter enemies. "Father, forgive them," He petitioned, "for they do not know what they do" (Luke 23:34). Christ's agonized prayer on their behalf was indeed answered in many of their lives. Later on, at the preaching of Peter and Paul, many repented and were forgiven.

While the best of us would have easily given up on such seemingly hopeless enemies, Christ would not. He is "not willing that any should perish but that all should come to repentance" (2 Peter 3:9). None of us has ever been mistreated as Jesus was. But isn't His example a great incentive to join Him in praying for those who mistreat and persecute us, even for those who abuse us the most? Jesus found in this malicious mistreatment of the very ones He came to save an opportunity to pray for them. From our perspective such people may appear beyond hope, but Christ's intercessory prayer on the cross assures us that there is hope even for the most hopeless. Only Christ's mighty intercessions could transform such from implacable enemies to loyal friends.

FREE ACCESS

When Jesus cried "It is finished," He died and "the veil of the temple was torn in two from top to bottom" (Mark 15:38). The torn veil to the Most Holy Place represents Christ's broken body tearing asunder any human inaccessibility to God's presence. That torn veil of Christ's broken body freely connects humanity with divinity, giving us free access into the presence of God. That is why the apostle Paul challenges us to "come boldly to the throne of grace, that we may obtain mercy and find grace to help in time of need" (Heb. 4:16). Also God who made us alive with His Son, "made us sit together in the heavenly places in Christ Jesus" (Eph. 2:5, 6). In Jesus, our trustworthy friend and mighty intercessor, "we have boldness and access with confidence through faith in Him" (Eph. 3:12).

Intercessory prayer is never a human invention, for it issues forth from the heart of God. In Ezekiel 22:30 God searches for a person to come before Him to intercede, but He sadly returns empty-handed. He declares: "So I sought for a man among them who would make a wall, and stand in the gap before Me on behalf of the land, that I should not destroy it; but I found no one." What a letdown! For the all-searching God to find no one. Yet even when on earth He finds no one, He always finds one in His Son Jesus, who ever "lives to make intercession for us" (Heb. 7:25).

MICHAEL'S MIGHTY HELP

There is an unusual reference in the Old Testament to Christ's engagement in Daniel's intercessory prayer. In Daniel 10:11-13 a mysterious curtain is pulled back to reveal a glimpse of what transpires behind the scenes, unseen by human eyes, in response to our sincere prayers. For 21 days Daniel had been humbling himself in earnest prayer for his people's return from the exile. While wondering if God was going to respond, the angel Gabriel arrived and informed him that even from the first day of his intercession his words were heard and Gabriel was there because of them.

During those 21 days the evil forces were busily working on the mind of the Persian king to dissuade him from releasing the Hebrew exiles. What an intense war that must have been. Finally, after three weeks, Michael (Christ) joined the struggle and assisted Gabriel in contending with the demonic powers at work. Of course, we cannot fathom all the issues involved in this great controversy between good and evil. We do not know exactly why the mighty Gabriel needed the assistance of the mighty Intercessor. Yet we are certain that the preincarnate Christ was even then personally involved in answering prayers and gaining victories. It is a biblical fact that it worked then and that it still works today.

Believer in Christ, never think for a moment that you are alone when you pray! All of heaven, with all its rich resources, is on your side. Gabriel, the glorious angel who stands in the very presence of God, is by your side. The eternal Son of God is always there as your tenacious mighty intercessor.

A TREMENDOUS BOOST

It should give us such a boost to realize that Jesus is always engaged in our prayer life. When we grow weary He never tires, when we slumber He never falls asleep, and when we forget He always remembers. Thank God that even when He searches for a man to intercede and finds no one, we are sufficiently covered because He always finds one in Jesus. When our prayers seem inadequate, His prayers are all-effective. When our pleas appear sluggish, His pleas are all-fervent. When all our righteousness is as filthy rags, He is "The Lord Our Righteousness" (Jer. 23:6). And when our prayers seem unavailing, His are much availing.

I don't know about you, but whenever I read the last part of the promise in James 5:16, I would get discouraged about my prayers. "The effective, fervent prayer of a righteous man avails much." My fervency and faith are not strong, like Elijah's or Paul's. My righteousness seems so small in comparison to Enoch's or Noah's. Conclusion: If there is little righteousness in me, there is little availing in my prayers. That was my demoralizing dilemma, but what was the solution? Work on my righteousness? No. Work on my faith and fervency? Again, no. The supernatural solution for me was to focus on Christ's faith, fervency, and perfect righteousness. Behold Him "The Lord Our Righteousness."

The context of James 5:13-18 speaks about church members praying for each other. Yet when it comes to my prayer life, it greatly helps me to view my fervency, effectiveness, and availing in the framework of Christ's all-sufficiency. With my righteousness as filthy rags, I must have His spotless robe of righteousness. Therefore I can correctly say of Christ: the fervent prayer of the Righteous Man avails much. And when He becomes my righteousness, my prayers become availing in His availing prayers. The pure robe of His righteousness is all-pervasive and must indeed cover everything about me—even my prayers. This point is crucial in revitalizing our prayer life, and we will come back to it in the next chapter.

My heartfelt testimony is that the Lord may open my eyes to see the same Jesus, who fervently prayed for His disciples and enemies, pray for me today. I gaze at His divine arm grasping the throne of God on my behalf. I hear the pounding of His nailed-scarred hand on heaven's gate for such a sinner as I. I tremble at the fervency of His powerful petitions, engulfing my faint attempts at petitioning. Praise God that I am clothed with the robe of His righteousness and the fervency and effectiveness of His intercessions. Praise God for giving me the assurance and security that I am accepted in the Beloved, covered in His atoning blood. In Him all is well with my soul.

Discussion Questions

1. Analyze this statement further: "Touching a trickle of cool water can be refreshing, but how much better to plunge into the rushing torrents of a mighty river."

2. What is the closest experience you would describe as being a prayer of sweat, blood, and tears? What relationship exists between intensity in prayer and prevailing in prayer?

3. From your own perspective, how do you relate to this statement: "No time to pray, no time to breathe, no time to live"? To what extent have you experienced the truth of this?

4. Jesus prayed for Peter and Mary. With whom would you identify more? Why?

5. Christ prayed fervently for His tormentors. Think of a person whom you may consider an "enemy." What do you think would happen if you earnestly prayed for him or her?

6. What particular challenges do you have that you desire Jesus to fit into His intercessions?

7. Christ's body was broken to give you access into the Most Holy of the heavenly sanctuary. What barriers need to be broken down in your life so that you can avail yourself of the benefits of Christ's intercessions? How does the cross make this possible for you?

8. Christ's perfect righteousness covers your righteousness as well as your prayers. Explain.

CHAPTER FIVE

He Prays With Us

*"Then another angel, having a golden censer, came and
stood at the altar. He was given much incense, that he should
offer it with the prayers of the saints upon the golden altar which
was before the throne. And the smoke of
the incense, with the prayers of the saints, ascended before
God from the angel's hand" (Revelation 8:3, 4).*

Niagara Falls is one of the most magnificent natural
wonders in North America. The Niagara River
flows from Lake Erie, and about halfway on its course to
Lake Ontario it plunges into the falls. Its spectacular beauty
attracts millions of tourists annually. What a wondrous and
irresistible sight to behold! When I first laid my eyes on it,
not only was I enchanted by its wondrous beauty, I was
seized by the spiritual insights it yielded—insights that pro-
foundly influenced my prayer life.

On my first visit I gazed transfixed at the mighty flow
of the American Niagara Falls. At such a close range I took
it all in! I saw its terrific torrents, I heard its howling thun-
der, and felt its tumultuous power. I could not pull myself
away from the sight, and found myself totally overwhelmed by God's abundant love and power. As I was
earnestly praying for guidance, and for a prevailing prayer
life, He vividly impressed upon my mind that this contin-

uous mighty flow of the Niagara Falls represents Christ's powerful prayers for me. "Yes, Lord," I said, "but this is about Christ's mighty prayers. What about my weak prayers? They are like a few droplets of water, at best only a trickle." Then conviction hit me like a thunderbolt: "Why not join your weak prayers to His mighty prayers?"

Much Water and Much Incense

All along I felt that my faith was feeble and my prayers were puny, but now the Lord was directing my mind to look not to self but to the Savior. He was clearly telling me not to focus on my faith and prayers but on His. To rivet my shaky faith in His solid faith, to join my measly prayers with His mighty prayers. Take the plunge, go with the flow, was the conviction of my heart. Whenever I pray Christ wants me to anchor my mustard-seed faith in His giant faith, and to join my trickle of prayers with the mighty flow of the Niagara Falls of His prevailing prayers. This perspective on prayer became my answer to a closer walk with Him.

The Spirit's conviction to join my puny prayers with Christ's powerful prayers led me to study Revelation 8:3 and 4. The clear context of this passage is the crucial subject of prayer. The use of words like "censer," "altar," "incense," "prayers," "throne," and "smoke" makes this clear. In addition, such activity occurs in the vicinity of the altar of incense before the inner veil leading to God's glory. How wonderful to see such unmistakable indicators of prayer endeavors taking place in the heavenly sanctuary. Here the curtain is pulled aside to give us a rare glimpse of how the prayers of the saints are processed. The angel, who stands by the altar of incense, was given much incense and instructed to offer it with the prayers of all the saints. And he did offer up this mixture of incense and prayers upon the golden altar, right in front of God's throne.

It is evident that this passage is dealing with two separate entities that become mixed together as one: the much incense and the saints' prayers. This fact is also obvious in verse four of our passage: "And the smoke of the incense, with the prayers of the saints, ascended before God from the angel's hand." Here we have the two entities again becoming one: the smoke of the burning incense intermingled with our prayers, ascending together to God.

As I studied this passage, I was reminded of my Niagara Falls experience. The trickle of my prayers mixed with the flood of Christ's prayers sounds like the puny prayers of the saints mingled with the much incense of Christ's perfect righteousness and intercession. Prior to this realization, I would always feel that my prayer was hanging by a thin thread. But now it is radically different. My thin thread of prayer is interwoven with the firm fabric of His prayers.

What an awesome privilege! Now I can pray with my greatest Prayer Partner, Jesus. His "much incense" fragrances my odorous prayers tainted with self. Now I am irresistibly drawn to come boldly before the throne of grace, knowing that my best prayers and petitions must be consumed by the purging fire of Christ's perfect righteousness, and fragranced by the incense of His intercessions wafting above the mercy seat.

THE EMBLEM OF HIS MEDIATION

Even in the Old Testament, "while the people of God

were without, earnestly praying, the incense kindled by the holy fire was to arise before God *mingled* with their prayers. This incense was an *emblem* of the mediation of Christ" (*Temperance,* p. 43; italics supplied). The incense represents at least two things: Christ's perfect mediation and His perfect righteousness. "These prayers [of ours], mingled with the incense of the perfection of Christ, will ascend as fragrance to the Father, and answers will come" (*Testimonies,* vol. 6, p. 467). Here the type of Exodus 30:7 and 8 meets the antitype of Revelation 8:3 and 4. Aaron, the earthly high priest, was to burn incense upon the altar of incense before the mercy seat every morning and evening for "perpetual incense" before the Lord. Jesus, our heavenly high priest, with His "much incense" perpetually makes intercession for us before the mercy seat.

It is interesting to note that Aaron was to burn incense on the altar every morning and evening. Our prayers ascending with the prayers of Jesus must be a daily experience, fresh every morning, carrying us through to each evening. It is not something sporadic that occurs now and then, but something indispensable that we breathe perpetually. "Unceasing prayer is the unbroken union of the soul with God, so that the life from God flows into our life; and from our life, purity and holiness flow back to God" (*Steps to Christ,* p. 98). But offering prayer mixed with incense on a daily basis implies not only perpetuity but also priority. Our utmost priority is to begin and conclude every day with God, breathing His Spirit throughout the day.

God's people in Christ's day were found praying at the very time when priest Zacharias was in the Temple burning incense (Luke 1:10). From their earliest history they associated the ascending smoke of the burning incense upon the golden altar with their prayers ascending above the inner veil unto the mercy seat. "The incense, ascending with the prayers of Israel, represents the merits and intercessions of Christ, His perfect righteousness, which through faith is imputed to His people, and which can alone make the worship of sinful beings acceptable to God. . . . They united in silent prayer, with their faces toward the holy place. Thus *their petitions ascended with the cloud of incense,* while faith laid hold upon the merits of the promised Saviour prefigured by the atoning sacrifice" (*Patriarchs and Prophets,* p. 353; italics supplied).

Revelation 5:8 gives us another glimpse into the incense of prayer: "Now when He [Christ the Lamb] had taken the scroll, the four living creatures and the twenty-four elders fell down before the Lamb, each having a harp, and golden bowls full of incense, which are the prayers of the saints." Our humble prayers are in the holy environs of the heavenly sanctuary where the slain Lamb intercedes for us. What great encouragement this is! Apparently God regards such prayers as very precious in His sight. They are described as incense contained in golden bowls. Christ's merits and intercessions are also described as incense, which leads us to conclude that the "much incense" of His prayers is mingled with the incense of our prayers.

The Holy Spirit descended upon a group of Advent believers during a season of prayer in Topsham, Maine, in 1847. Ellen White was present and was taken in vision and shown the glories of heaven. Jesus was her personal Guide, and He opened the apartments of the heavenly sanctuary to her. Here is an excerpt of the vision describing when she was taken into the Holy of Holies: "Jesus stood by the ark, and as the saints' prayers came up to Him, the incense in the censer would smoke, and He would *offer up their prayers with the smoke of the incense* to His Father" (*Early Writings,* p. 32; italics supplied).

SWEET AROMA

The apostles Paul and John use similar powerful imagery to depict divine human cooperation in prayer and witness. Paul admonishes us to walk in the love of Christ, who "has loved us and given Himself for us, an offering and a sacrifice to God for a sweet-smelling aroma" (Eph. 5:2). Here we have Paul depicting Christ Himself as the burning sacrifice exuding a sweet aroma unto God. And in 2 Corinthians 2:14 and 15 he describes us as the aroma of Christ, diffusing His sweet fragrance always and everywhere. Paul has in mind the powerful analogy of a Roman triumphal procession, where a victorious general would be welcomed by many dignitaries, some carrying censers brimming with sweet burning incense.

So in the passages from Ephesians and Corinthians, Paul makes use of the imagery of burning sacrifice and burning incense, not only to describe Christ's ministry but also our joint role in it. We walk in Christ's love of offering Himself as a burning sacrifice. And we march in Christ's victory of diffusing the sweet burning incense of His knowledge. As we give ourselves to God in uniting with Jesus' intercessions, we too present our "bodies a living sacrifice, holy, acceptable to God" (Rom. 12:2). Walking in His love and diffusing His sweet fragrance becomes such an all-absorbing way of life that Paul even calls us the aroma of Christ. Compare this with how John in Revelation 8:3, 4 aptly describes the "much incense" of Christ's intercession mingling with the prayers of all the saints, and ascending as sweet-smelling smoke before God. How glorious it is that Christ desires our wholehearted co-operation and partnership in this sacred ministry!

AS MUCH AS HE LOVES HIS SON

Some may wonder why Jesus needs to pray for us and with us before God. Jesus' prayers are not to appease God or to make Him love us as His Son does. The Father's love for us is eternal, and His deep concern for our salvation is inexhaustible. He loves us with the same love as He loves His only Son, for that is why He was willing to go to the extreme extent of giving Him up for us. Jesus, in His last prayer for His disciples, made this wonderful truth clear: "I in them, and You in Me; that they may be made perfect in one, and that the world may know that You have sent Me, and have loved them as You have loved Me" (John 17:23). God looks from His throne of grace and sees us covered in His Son's righteousness. He accepts us in His Beloved, making us His own sons and daughters, opening wide His vast storehouse of grace and redemption.

Consider the close relationship between God's love for us and His Son's intercession on our behalf, as seen in these statements: "The Father demonstrates His infinite love for Christ, who paid our ransom with His blood, by receiving and *welcoming Christ's friends as His friends*. He is satisfied with the atonement made. He is glorified by the incarnation, the life, death, and mediation of His Son" (*Testimonies,* vol. 6, p. 364; italics supplied). Furthermore, in doing this "He [Christ] gathers into [His] censer the prayers, the praise, and the confessions of His people, and with these He puts His own spotless righteousness. Then, perfumed with the merits of Christ's propitiation, the incense comes up before God wholly and entirely acceptable. Then gracious answers are returned" (*The Seventh-day Adventists Bible Commentary,* Ellen G. White Comments, vol. 6, p. 1078).

So Jesus prays for us and with us not for the sake of convincing God to love us. The Father has been completely convinced of that from the foundation of the world. However, the whole universe is watching with keen interest to see how the drama of the great controversy is being played out on the theater of Planet Earth. Therefore Jesus voluntarily opens Himself up and invites the watching universe to gaze into God's character, to see for themselves what is involved in the salvation of humanity.

Joint Venture With Christ

When it comes to prevailing prayer, the focus is not on our prayer but on the praying Jesus. What a blessed relief! We do not know how to pray as we ought. Our stammering words tainted by our sinful humanity are certainly inadequate. Our mixed motives seep out of our self-centered heart. Our prayer life desperately needs to be *linked* to the prayer life of our Savior. Our unadorned prayers yearn to be fragranced with the smoke of Christ's sweet incense in the heavenly sanctuary, consumed with the holy fire from the altar. By necessity Christ mingles His perfect intercessions with our prayers because the best of them are tainted with our humanity. They need the cleansing work of His incense as they ascend to God (see *Selected Messages,* book 1, p. 344).

One of the most helpful insights on this subject is found in *The Desire of Ages.* I identify with the disciples and receive Christ's words for them as if spoken directly to me. "He [Jesus] explained that the secret of their success would be in asking for strength and grace in His name. He would be present before the Father to make request for them. The prayer of the humble suppliant He presents as His own desire in that soul's behalf. Every sincere prayer is heard in heaven. It may not be fluently expressed; but if the heart is in it, it will ascend to the sanctuary where Jesus ministers, and He will present it to the Father without one awkward, stammering word, *beautiful and fragrant with the incense* of His own perfection" (p. 667; italics supplied).

It is an honor when a person, mighty in prayer, invites me to join him in praying for others. But how much greater an honor it is when Jesus, our Mighty Intercessor, longs for us to join Him in praying for others! He not only prays passionately for us, but wants us to join Him in His prayers, to go with the flow of His intercessions.

CHRIST'S PRAYER VIGIL

In the previous chapter we studied how Jesus prayed for Peter. Shortly after that experience, we see Jesus in the Garden of Gethsemane appealing to Peter by name to stay awake and pray with Him. Finding His three disciples asleep, He pointedly asked Peter: "Simon, are you sleeping? Could you not watch one hour?" (Mark 14:37). It is significant that Jesus mentioned neither John nor James by name, but only Peter. I believe it was because of the recent experience of Jesus praying for him not to fail in his faith (Luke 22:32). Jesus desired reciprocity, and wanted to engage Peter in His prayer life. He needed him and the disciples to "stay here and watch with Me" (Matt. 26:38).

The word "watch" is significant here because it refers to the disciples staying awake for the purpose of sharing in Christ's prayer vigil. It is remarkable that the Mighty Intercessor, who prayed many times for His disciples, now needs them to join Him in His own prayer. What an enormous privilege they squandered in failing to share this most sacred hour with their Master. If they had taken advantage of this special occasion, they would have been braced for the terrible trials just ahead of them. Can Jesus count on us when He desires to share a prayer burden that is upon His travailing heart? Or does He entreat us to enter into His supplications only to find us slumbering?

When Christ lays one of His prayer burdens upon our hearts, it is a holy calling of the highest order. This is a clear indication that He trusts us with the burdens on His heart, that He desires to pull us close to Him in approaching the mercy seat. It is interesting to note that Peter and John, who failed to join Jesus in prayer at Gethsemane, describe the believers (along with themselves) as priests unto God through Christ. "You also, as living stones, are being built up a spiritual house, a holy priesthood, to offer up sacrifices acceptable to God through Jesus Christ" (1 Peter 2:5). John writes about this priesthood ministry in Christ, who "has made us kings and priests" unto His Father (Rev. 1:6).

PRIESTS WITH OUR HIGH PRIEST

Christ our High Priest has made us priests in Him. He

has ordained us to offer spiritual sacrifices of prayers, petitions, and supplications through Him. That is why praying with Jesus makes so much sense. We are called to enter into this priestly ministry of weeping with Jesus and sharing in His travail for others. "Blessed are they also *who weep with Jesus* in sympathy with the world's sorrow and in sorrow for its sin. . . . All who are followers of Christ will *share* in this experience. As they *partake* of His love they will *enter into His travail* for the saving of the lost." Then there is the promise of His joy and glory to those who share in His travail for the lost. "They share in the sufferings of Christ, and they will share also in the glory that shall be revealed. *One with Him* in His work, drinking with Him the cup of sorrow, they are partakers also of His joy" (*Thoughts From the Mount of Blessing,* pp. 12, 13; italics supplied).

How does our priesthood as believers in Christ interface with His high priestly ministry when it comes to prayer? Such holy participation always ensues from our unreserved and total submission to Him. For when He abides on the throne of our hearts, His life becomes our life. He lives in us and ministers through us. He loves, cares, sacrifices, affirms, and prays through us. Jesus ever lives to intercede for us. And as He ever lives in our lives, He ever prays in and through our lives. Our sanctified lives become an expression of His life.

It is our awesome privilege and sacred duty to serve as priests of intercession, even clothed with Christ's priestly vestments: "As we acknowledge before God our appreciation of Christ's merits, *fragrance is given to our intercessions.* Oh, who can value this great mercy and love! As we approach God through the virtue of Christ's merits, we are *clothed with*

His priestly vestments. He places us close by His side, encircling us with His human arm, while with His divine He
grasps the throne of the Infinite. He puts His merits, as
sweet incense, in a censer in our hands, in order to encourage our petitions." (*The Seventh-day Adventist Bible
Commentary,* Ellen G. White Comments, vol. 6, p. 1078;
italics supplied).

This priesthood of all believers was demonstrated in
the experience of Job praying for his children as well as for
his critics. He consecrated his children to God and sacrificed and prayed for them regularly (Job 1:4, 5). In fact,
Job in his priestly role was a type of Jesus our High Priest
praying for us. Job sacrificed and prayed regularly for his
children, and so did Jesus when He sacrificed Himself and
now lives to pray for us. Moreover, God wanted Job to intercede for his three critics. "My servant Job shall pray for
you," God said to them. "For I will accept him, lest I deal
with you according to your folly" (Job 42:8).

Jesus also interceded for His critics and tormentors that
God would forgive them. In a sense, Job entered the sacred realm of Jesus' travail and intercessions for friend and
foe alike. As consecrated believers we stand as priests before God—in Christ our High Priest. Like Job, are we entering on a regular basis Christ's holy realm of intercession
for others? It is our privilege and sacred duty to do so.

The Israelites feared for their lives because they had re-
fused to have God rule over them. Notice what the
prophet Samuel said about the indispensable ministry of
intercession when the people asked him to pray for them.
"Moreover, as for me, far be it from me that I should sin
against the Lord in ceasing to pray for you" (1 Sam. 12:19,

23). He viewed his priestly prayers for them as so crucially important that he considered it a sin against God not to do so. How often do we consider our failure to enter the realm of Christ's intercessions for others as a sin against God? Yet according to His Word, this is so. As alluded to earlier, we who are followers of Christ "will share in this experience [of weeping with Jesus in sorrow for the sinful world]" (*Thoughts From the Mount of Blessing,* pp. 12, 13).

BLOT ME OUT!

We briefly touched on the example of Job and Samuel in entering Christ's sacred realm of intercession. But for me the most powerful example of Christ's intercession is found in the ministry of Moses in behalf of God's wayward people. God wanted to be left to destroy the stubborn bunch for their great rebellion in worshiping the golden calf. But He assured His servant Moses that He would make a new and mighty nation out of his seed. However, Moses was not thinking about himself now, but was consumed with concern about the people. Spontaneously he began to review to God the wonderful promises He had given them. And then he went up to the Lord on the mountain to make atonement for their sins. In his prayer of intercession Moses earnestly pleaded with God: "Oh, these people have sinned a great sin, and have made for themselves a god of gold! Yet now, if You will forgive their sin—but if not, I pray, blot me out of Your book which You have written" (Ex. 32:31, 32).

In the councils of the Trinity, the Son of God volunteered to give His life for the world. It would be at a tremendous cost: experiencing the second death on behalf of sinful and lost humanity. Moses' offer that his name be blotted out of the book of life was not accepted by God, but Christ's offer was indeed accepted. Jesus experienced the second death; His name was blotted out from the book of life. And in that generous divine act, neither Moses' name nor any name needs ever to be blotted out. Certainly Moses' earnest intercession, flowing from a heart of love, enters into that sacred realm of Christ's intercession for fallen humanity.

How awesome it would be to experience such quality of intercession for others! It would enduringly unite our hearts with the heart of Jesus for a dying world. Can you imagine for a moment how God felt when He realized that His servant Moses was willing to give his life—not just his temporal life but his eternal life—for that rebellious lot? A totally selfless act. Now, can you imagine Him looking at your heart and mine and ascertaining in us the same spirit of ultimate sacrifice? This is at the essence of having His mind and reflecting His character.

The prayer of Stephen for those stoning him may be considered the closest to that of Christ's prayer for those crucifying Him. He too entered that sacred realm of Christ's ministry of intercession. "Then he knelt down and cried out with a loud voice, 'Lord, do not charge them with this sin.' And when he had said this, he fell asleep" (Acts 7:60). It is difficult to pray for those who are critical of us, but how much more difficult to pray for those who are literally killing us. It is impossible to do this without God first transforming our hearts to be more like the heart of Jesus. Then we too can pray sincerely as Stephen did. Stephen's prayer for those stoning him was modeled after Christ's prayer for those crucifying Him. And when we become established in Christ, our hearts can beat together with His heart—for even our worst enemies. This type of praying is a sure sign that Christ has become our solid anchor.

WE BELIEVE FOR YOU

There is an unusual reference to intercession in Mark 2:5. It is recorded that "when Jesus saw their faith, He said to the paralytic, 'Son, your sins are forgiven you.'" When Jesus healed people, He commented on their faith. But here He referred to the faith of the four faithful friends. Friends who were determined by any means—even breaking through the roof—to bring the paralytic to Jesus. The fact that this man was carried by his friends on a bed indicates that he was totally helpless. His friends had to encourage him and to believe for him, yet Jesus accepted their faith in his behalf. Ellen White counsels a despondent woman weak in faith to hold on to the hand of Jesus. "I know that the Lord loves you. If you cannot rely upon your own faith, rely upon the faith of others. We believe and hope for you. *God accepts our faith in your behalf*" (*Testimonies,* vol. 2, p. 319; italics supplied).

Isn't it amazing how much God tries to help us? If someone is so weak that he or she cannot believe, Jesus allows us to believe for that one. And if it makes such a difference to pray and believe for that one, how much more availing are the prayers of Jesus when He, the anchor of our faith, believes for us. I will never forget the television images of a struggling flight attendant trying to hold on to the life preserver that was lowered by a rescue helicopter hovering above. Barely keeping her head above the chunks of ice, she would struggle to grasp that life pre-server, but by now all her strength was exhausted. A man on the shore, observing this horrific scene, plunged into the icy waters and helped this struggling woman to shore.

This world is full of such people who sense their need for Jesus, yet because of horrible circumstances they remain stuck in a slippery muddy mire of life. They desperately need the helping hands of friends who would connect them to the grasp of the Savior's hand. Allow such brands plucked from the fire to lean on you as you gradually lead them to lean on Jesus. Your caring, your faith, and your prayers become a living extension of the Lord's ministry.

JESUS IN OUR MIDST

Let us go back to Gethsemane for a moment. There Jesus needed a helping hand. Often He interceded for His disciples, but now He was offering intercessions for Himself. Into such an intimate, sacred hour He yearned to have His disciples enter. He longed to have them enter the holy realm of sharing in His own intercessions. During His prayer vigil, "He longed to know that they were praying for Him and for themselves. . . . Thus when the Saviour was most in need of their sympathy and prayers, they were found asleep. Even Peter was sleeping" (*The Desire of Ages,* pp. 687-689).

So far we have been focusing on Peter, but what about John? Why didn't the disciple whom Jesus loved stay awake to share this prayer vigil with Him, especially when his Master entreated him to do so several times? "His [John's] earnest prayers should have mingled with those of His loved Saviour in the time of His supreme sorrow" (*ibid.,* p. 689). And what about James, the third member of

71

Christ's inner circle? The same applies to him. Like the other two, his "spirit truly [was] ready, but the flesh [was] weak" (Mark 14:38, KJV). Our best avails nothing unless it avails with His best.

Just as Jesus reached out to His disciples to pray with Him, so He reaches out to us today. The same Jesus promises us: "For where two or three are gathered together in My name, I am there in the midst of them" (Matt. 18:20). The words "where" and "midst" in this text point to a place, a locality. And this locality is not on the sideline or in some corner, it is right there in the center of our prayer gathering. Jesus takes great delight in being at the center of our hearts and prayer circles when we come to God in prayer.

The Old Testament background for this important reference is found in Deuteronomy 17:6 and 19:5. There it refers to a judicial decision based on two or three witnesses. But in Matthew 18:20 the immediate context has to do with the church's God-given authority and responsibility to deal with an offending member. But then Jesus adds the reference to the disciples meeting in His name, and Him being in their midst. Meeting in Jesus' name implies a meeting where prayer is offered and Christ is in the center.

In a general sense Jesus always joins us when we pray in His name. He wraps His strong loving arm around us and draws us close to His heart. In Matthew 11:25-27, Jesus prays to the Father for His disciples, offering Himself as the only access to God. Then He immediately makes the invitation in verse 28: "Come to Me, all you who labor and are heavy laden, and I will give you rest." Only God can give us real help, and in Jesus alone we have access into His presence. Therefore it is indispensable for us not to wander here or there but to go directly to Him. How often we reach out to others but not to Jesus! We feel we are too sinful and needy to go directly and immediately to Jesus. But our tremendous need is exactly what qualifies us to go to Him. The more needy, the more qualified. He looks beyond our faults and sees our need; He specifically invites the weary and heavy laden to come to Him.

Come to Him as you are. Come with all your burdens and He will never cast you out. Linger in the embrace of the praying Jesus. He is joining you in prayer. He is making your burdens His own. Rest in the arms of the Prince of Peace. Rest in the assurance that no power can pluck you out of His hand.

QUESTIONS FOR DISCUSSION

1. Where are the golden altar and censer in the heavenly sanctuary? What is the significance of that location to our prayers? How is Christ's "broken body" related to "the inner veil"?

2. How does a focus on the "much incense"of Christ's perfect righteousness and intercession affect your prayer life? How does it boost your confidence level?

3. Why is it indispensable for Christ's "much incense" to fragrance our odorous prayers?

4. How is prayer a joint venture with Christ? What is His role and what is our role?

5. What valuable lessons can we draw from Bible intercessors like Moses, Job, Samuel, and Stephen? How can their examples help us enter the sacred realm of Christ's intercessions?

6. Jesus longed to have His three disciples join Him in His prayer vigil. But it was a struggle, since the "spirit was willing but the flesh is weak." Relate this to your prayer experience.

7. How does your belief in the "priesthood of all believers" help you enter the realm of Christ's high priestly ministry? What does it mean to you personally that He prays with you? Have you had an experience of believing for someone? Share it.

8. Why do we often go to someone else to help us in a crisis instead of going to Jesus?

CHAPTER SIX

Embraced by His Prayers

"And He said to him, 'Most assuredly, I say to you, hereafter you shall see heaven open, and the angels of God ascending and descending upon the Son of Man' " (John 1:51).

In this account in John 1, Nathaniel was thinking of a fig tree while Jesus was pointing his eyes toward heaven. Being seen under a fig tree fascinated him, but Jesus was about to expand his horizons to see an open heaven crowded with angels around the Son of man. All too often we, like Nathaniel, see trees instead of heaven, figs instead of stars, people instead of angels, ourselves instead of the Son of man. So frequently we compare ourselves to others instead of looking to Jesus, the Author and Finisher of our faith. We prejudge people and try to squeeze them into categories based on race, religion, relationships, or achievements.

In Nathaniel's story we clearly see how he misjudged Jesus simply because He came from Nazareth. "Can anything good come out of Nazareth?" (verse 46) was his initial assessment of Jesus. Notice the Lord's generous response and how it highlighted Nathaniel's potential: "Behold, an Israelite indeed, in whom is no deceit" (verse

47). In essence Nathaniel was saying of the Nazarene, "He is no good." But in contrast Christ was saying to him, "You are a good man." Christ's affirming words enlightened Nathaniel more about Him. He first viewed Him as no good, and then as an intelligent person, a respected teacher, and finally as the Son of God and the King of Israel (verses 48, 49). If in such a short time he was so inspired by Christ, imagine how his life was going to be transformed following his Master for years to come.

Here, in this engaging dialogue with Nathaniel, Jesus is clearly alluding to Jacob's ladder dream in Genesis 28:10-18. But in John 1:51, He specifically applies the mystical ladder to Himself: "Hereafter you shall see heaven open, and the angels of God ascending and descending upon the Son of Man." The ladder was the focal point of Jacob's dream that dreary night, connecting heaven with earth, divinity with humanity. Like Nathaniel, Jacob was looking at the earthly instead of the heavenly. Scheming with his mother, lying to his father, robbing his brother, and now running for his life in a hostile desert. Earthly blunders were pulling him down, almost drowning him under a load of guilt and fear.

FROM A PILLOW PRAYER TO A PILLAR PRAYER

Jacob the fugitive was braving the treacherous desert between his home in Beersheba and the unknown territory of Mesopotamia. Although dodging roving murderous bands and vicious wild beasts was fearsome, his inward burden of guilt was even heavier than his outward burden of fear. Jacob's troubled conscience was a mighty tyrant that separated him from his family, friends, and from God Himself.

Prayer was probably the least attractive thing for him to do, but it was the most important. Prayer is needed the most when desired the least. "God often brings people to a crisis to show them their own weakness and to point them to the Source of all strength. If they pray . . . their weak points will become their strong points" (*Christ Triumphant,* p. 89).

In his weakness and weariness, Jacob probably turned to God for some hint that he was not totally forsaken. Finding a stone for a pillow, he collapsed into an exhausted sleep. His hesitant prayer was probably for some assurance of God's care, and was answered in a marvelous manifestation of His presence. In his dream Jacob was shown a giant ladder. Its base was on the ground where he was, and its top reached to heaven where God is. Myriads of angels were ascending and descending on its steps. When he awoke, he confessed the awesomeness of God's presence. The house of God was right there where he stood, connecting him with the gate of heaven.

In God's awesome presence, Jacob's pillow became a pillar. A flat stone lost in the desert aptly represented Jacob's experience. But seeing heaven's open gate transformed that flat dry stone. Jacob stood it up and now that anointed stone pointed toward heaven. Although the anointed pillar did not reach far, yet it was pointing in the upward direction and lining up with the ladder. What do you have for a prayer? A pillow prayer or a pillar prayer? A pillow prayer does not go far, but in God's presence it becomes a pillar payer. It breaks out of its earthly confines and goes upward while clinging to and climbing upon the mystical ladder. It goes far—all the way to the gates of heaven where it lines up with Jesus, the mystical ladder.

Remember, Jesus' human arm is embracing us right here where we are, and yet His divine arm reaches the throne.

A PATHWAY OPENED

Praise God, Christ is that mystical ladder connecting finite humanity with infinite divinity. Jacob was hedged about with worry and anxiety, blinded by his limitations, but Christ opened his eyes, and he saw an open highway before him. "Worry is blind, and cannot discern the future; but Jesus sees the end from the beginning. In every difficulty He has His way prepared to bring relief. *Our heavenly Father has a thousand ways to provide for us, of which we know nothing*" (*The Desire of Ages*, p. 330; italics supplied). Jacob on his own would not have been able to see beyond his pillow experience. But Christ broke through the barriers coming down to his level to bring him up with Him to the throne of grace. "Christ is the ladder. . . . This is the ladder, the base of it resting upon the earth, the top reaching to the highest heavens. The broken links have been repaired. *A highway has been thrown up* along which the weary and heavy laden may pass. They may enter heaven and find rest" (*Christ Triumphant*, p. 87; italics supplied).

This is a wonderful illustration of Christ's high-priestly intercession for us in the sanctuary above. We were outside the gate, unreached by God because of our sins. We could not go through the veils and into His presence. Christ's arm is long enough to save and His ear is wide open to hear, but our prayers are blocked by our sins. "Behold, the Lord's hand is not shortened, that it cannot save; nor his ear heavy, that it cannot hear. But your iniquities have separated you from your God; and your sins have hidden His face from you, so that He will not hear" (Isa. 59:1, 2). Our human problem is separation. His divine solution is atonement.

The reality of "atonement" is the antithesis of separation, for it brings us back to at-one-ment with God. In desiring to restore our oneness with Him, Christ broke through that separation with His broken body and spilled blood. "While we were yet sinners, Jesus died for us." Indeed He experienced the ultimate separation referred to in the Bible as the second death. "For He made Him who knew no sin to be sin for us, that we might become the righteousness of God in Him" (2 Cor. 5:21). Christ in the veil of His humanity passed through all the veils, opening a path all the way to Calvary. Then through the sacrifice of His broken body, outside the gate, He took us with Him through all the veils into the glorious presence of God. Listen to the words of Paul about this pathway: "Therefore, brethren, having boldness to enter the Holiest by the blood of Jesus, by a new and living way which He consecrated for us, through the veil, that is, His flesh" (Heb. 10:19, 20).

"I AM THE WAY"

This living link is our lifeline to heaven, and without it we are desolate. That is why the adversary "seeks *continually* to *obstruct the way* to the mercy-seat, that we may not by earnest supplication and faith obtain grace and power to resist temptation" (*Steps to Christ,* p. 95; italics supplied). Satan may insinuate that we have strayed too far outside the gate of God's mercy. But Jesus was crucified outside the gate, with His best reaching our worst. "Therefore Jesus also, that

He might sanctify the people with His own blood, suffered outside the gate" (Heb. 13:12). The gospel is powerful enough to save the worst sinner who comes to Him. And as long as we clasp Christ's outstretched hand and walk with Him, His shed blood is His pledge to carry us from wherever we are all the way to God's mercy seat within the inner veil. He is our only way into God's presence.

As Jesus was ready to offer Himself up, He talked to His disciples about the way into the Father's presence. Thomas could not fathom this idea, and was unclear as to what the Master was saying about such a way. Jesus came right to the point: "I am the way, the truth, and the life. No one comes to the Father except through Me" (John 14:6). This is the eternal purpose of God: that through Jesus we find free and full access to the Father. When we attach ourselves to Him, we do not adhere to a philosophy about or a way to the Father, we adhere to Christ *the* Way. And the way is sure because Jesus promised never to leave us nor forsake us. The apostle Paul explains that this was God's intent all along "according to the eternal purpose which He accomplished in Christ Jesus our Lord, in whom we have boldness and access with confidence through faith in Him" (Eph. 3:11, 12). When Jesus rules supreme on the throne of our heart, He becomes our way, our truth, and our life.

GABRIEL AND MICHAEL AT WORK

The prophet Daniel was allowed to see a glimpse of how his intercessory prayer on behalf of his people fit into the intercessions of Michael, who is Christ. But even before Daniel's prayer was embraced by Michael's prayer, we notice that Daniel was embraced by His love. In Daniel 10:5 and 6 we learn that in response to his three weeks of fasting and prayer, the Son of God appeared to him in His glory. (He appeared in the same glorious manner to John in vision in Revelation 1:13-15.) Then the angel Gabriel spoke encouraging words from Christ. First of all, Daniel was assured of God's great love: "O Daniel, man greatly beloved" (Dan. 10:11, 19). Then Gabriel, who stands in the presence of God, told him that from the first day of his three-week prayer vigil he was heard, and that he had come because of his prayer (verse 12). The words, "O man greatly beloved," are repeated, along with the assuring exhortation: "Fear not! Peace be to you; be strong, yes, be strong!" (verse 19).

Daniel was beginning to wonder about God's promises. He needed reassurance that He cared and that his prayers were being heard. He pressed his case for 21 days, wondering where God was in all of this. Yet in the midst of his bewilderment, Daniel was embraced by Heaven. What a valuable lesson to learn and remember. Although we do not always sense God's presence, and sometimes have no tangible indication of our prayers being answered, yet there is activity behind the scenes. Gabriel from the very presence of God is promptly on the scene. Christ in His glory appears. And Daniel is surrounded by God's great love that overcomes his fear and gives him peace and strength. Finally Michael Himself joins the fray to help Gabriel contend with the evil forces battling over the mind of Cyrus. Whenever the name "Michael" is used in the Bible, it always involves direct conflict with Satan and his forces who are arrayed against God's people.

As we have seen, many invisible forces are active as God brings this great controversy to a final conclusion. We must always keep this in mind whenever we pray. No matter how we feel, God's mighty forces are at work demolishing Satan's strongholds. And through all of this we are more than conquerors through Christ who loves us. No matter what, we will ultimately have the victory in Christ. And in the meantime, we are held in the embrace of Heaven.

Often we think that our human situation is all that is on Christ's mind. While we may be the focus of His care and attention, the whole universe is on His mind as well. He embraces the vast universe—not just us—in His love. In contending and interceding for us, He takes into consideration all the issues that affect our future, the plan of salvation, and the universe. For example, Michael was not only thinking of Daniel's immediate need of the Hebrew remnant returning to the earthly Jerusalem; He was also thinking of His final remnant going to the heavenly Jerusalem. As Jesus helps us, He is also dealing with vital issues in the great controversy. It gives me great comfort and courage to know that He is all-loving, all-wise, and all-powerful—able to balance everything out for our best and for the welfare of His vast creation.

Our wonderful Lord surrounds us with His loving embrace as we pray. He wants us to trust Him as we come into His presence. Like a loving father or mother, He longs to surround us with His compassionate and protective arms. And in that embrace, we are on the mind and in the heart of Jesus, our impregnable refuge. "Through sincere prayer we are brought into connection with the mind of the Infinite. We may have no remarkable evidence at the time that the face of our Redeemer is bending over us in compassion and love, *but this is even so.* We may not feel His visible touch, but *His hand is upon us* in love and pitying tenderness" (*Steps to Christ,* p. 97; italics supplied).

The points we have covered thus far fit into this embrace of Jesus' mighty prayers. Let's review them for a moment. His Niagara Falls prayer embraces our trickle of a prayer. His "much incense" of prayer fragrances our odorous prayer. His colossal ladder of prayer embraces our small pillar of prayer. Prayer means reaching beyond ourselves to God. And in Jesus we have the mighty one, the mystical ladder, to cling to and to climb upon. He embraces our prayer requests and makes them His very own. He broke through all the barriers with His broken body. Embracing us, He carries us back to God, giving us access into His presence. He pulled us up from the gutter of the outer court and made us to sit next to Him in heavenly places.

HIS EMBRACE IN PRAYER

Christ's compassionate and mighty arms embrace and connect our trembling prayers with the very gates of heaven. What could be more assuring than to know that Christ is embracing us when we earnestly pray? If it is a source of encouragement to have a loved one draw close to us and grasp our hand in prayer, how much more so for Christ to draw near us and embrace us with His compassionate and mighty arms. "As we acknowledge before God our appreciation of Christ's merits, fragrance is given to our intercessions. As we approach God through the virtue of the Redeemer's merits, Christ places us *close by His side,* encircling us with *His human arm,* while with *His divine arm* He grasps the throne of the Infinite. He puts His merits, as sweet incense, in the censer in our hands, in order to encourage our petitions. He promises to hear and answer our supplications. Yes, Christ has become the *medium* of prayer between God and man" (*Testimonies,* vol. 8, p. 178; italics supplied).

So whenever we join Christ in prayer:

1. Our sincere prayers are fragranced by Christ's merits and intercessions.

2. Christ draws close to us when we pray.

3. He encircles us with His human arm (representing His caring, love, and compassion).

4. With His divine arm He grasps the Infinite (representing His mighty power).

5. Christ Himself becomes the medium of prayer between us and God.

In order to make a vivid and lasting impression on our souls whenever we pray, why not demonstrate the important points of this promise with a friend? Illustrate this by drawing close to your friend, placing one arm around his or her shoulders, and raising your other arm toward heaven. Remember, now, that this is what Christ does when we pray.

Thus the Father accepts us when He sees us embraced in His Beloved Son. He receives and welcomes us as His friends because we are His Son's friends. For "no sooner does the child of God approach the mercy seat than he becomes the *client* of the great Advocate. At his first utterance of penitence and appeal for pardon Christ *espouses* his case and makes it His own, presenting the supplication before the Father *as His own request"* (*Testimonies,* vol. 6, p. 364; italics supplied).

It is impossible for us to encircle all the needs of others with sufficient and lasting help, but Jesus cares and He can. With His compassionate human arm He is able to encompass all our needs and petitions. He draws them close to His heart, and then causes them to ascend upon His mighty divine arm all the way to God's throne. In the embrace of the praying Jesus, our fragrant petitions are not left to themselves. They ascend higher and higher, unobstructed by obstacles, until they reach their heavenly destination. We need never fear that our prayers do not rise above the ceiling. For they ascend upon the divine arm, burst through the roof, clouds, and cosmos, not stopping until they reach the heavenly altar of incense. There Christ, our "medium of prayer," presents our prayers mixed with the sweet incense of His perfect righteousness and mighty intercessions.

DIVINE AVAILABILITY

So many in the political and corporate world vie for coveted access to the top echelons of leaders and executives. Some would do virtually whatever it takes to secure such access. Having access means having power and influence. And having free access implies unlimited power and influence. In Christ we have free and unlimited access to the throne of God. Free access to the Leader of the whole universe! No lobbying activity or peddling influence is ever needed. The priceless blood of Christ was spilled as the ultimate price for this pathway.

So what hinders us from experiencing this precious access? The apostle Paul urges us to profit from it when he writes: "We have boldness and access with confidence through faith in Him" (Eph. 3:12). The engulfing embrace of Christ infuses us with courage and boldness to access the Divine Presence. This daily experience captivates and captures our souls, and our trust in God develops so that we may daily dwell in His presence and breathe His Spirit.

HIS EMBRACE IN SUFFERING

This may sound too good to be true. Where is that free access to the power of God when in our suffering He seems so far away? Who can bridge the widening chasm we feel opening up before us—a gulf that seems to tear such free access away? Are we still in the loving embrace of His mighty prayers when we hurt so much? It is easy to feel Him near in our triumphs, but where is He in our tribulations? The good news is that no matter how our feelings fluctuate, no matter what the circumstances may be, we are kept tightly in that embrace, even more so in adversity than in prosperity. God—like a loving parent—stays especially close to His children when sickness or tragedy strikes. "The Father's presence encircled Christ. . . . He who is imbued with the Spirit of Christ abides in Christ. The blow that is aimed at him falls upon the Saviour, who surrounds him with His presence" (*Thoughts From the Mount of Blessing*, p. 71).

As mentioned earlier, our infinite God takes the long look, He surveys the total spectrum of reality. He is too wise to err, too loving not to do His utmost for us. In our finiteness we see only a tiny sliver of the circle of total reality. Even this tiny speck is shrouded in ignorance in comparison to the dazzling light of His infinite and perfect wisdom. Furthermore, all His wisdom merged with His infinite love is actively at work for us. His brilliant mind is never far from His compassionate heart. His wise acts always spring forth from His big and loving heart.

THE GREATEST ANSWERED PRAYER

A friend of ours was valiantly battling terminal cancer. Hit with this severe crisis, he remained cheerful and upbeat. We often prayed for his healing, but it seemed to be to no avail. In our fervent prayers we assured him that the embrace of the praying and healing Christ always connected him with God's throne. We earnestly believed that Christ in His boundless love and wisdom had the best answer for his problem. We availed ourselves continuously and completely of what He already desired to do in this critical situation. Yet despite all of this he was not physically healed.

I will never forget his comments when I visited with him and tried to encourage him. He calmly explained that even if he was never healed miraculously, God had already healed him spiritually. Even if our prayer requests for him would never be answered in the way we desired, he believed that his loving God had already answered his greatest prayer request. Saving his soul from eternal loss was the best answer he could ever receive, and anything else was secondary. He testified that God had used this trial to pull him out of a sinful lifestyle and to give him the assurance of eternal salvation. He believed that he would spend all of eternity in perfect health, and that he had confidence that he would be able to look back and praise God for his ordeal. God used this severe trial to give him eternal life.

And he would choose cancer any day rather than lose out on eternal life! In the meantime he would continue praising Him, knowing that through both triumph and trial he was embraced by His love. For what is thought of as trial now would prove to be supreme triumph then.

His testimony continued: He often contemplated the supreme sufferings of Christ for his redemption, and realized that what he was facing was so small in comparison. He thought also that it was a special honor for him to share a little bit in Christ's suffering. He remembered that "the sufferings of this present time are not worthy to be compared with the glory which shall be revealed in us" (Rom. 8:18). He also recalled that "God never leads His children otherwise than they would choose to be led, if they knew the end from the beginning, and discern the glory of the purpose which they are fulfilling as coworkers with Him. . . . 'Unto you it is given in the behalf of Christ, not only to believe on Him, but also to suffer for His sake' (Phil. 1:29). And of all the gifts that Heaven can bestow upon men, fellowship with Christ in His sufferings is *the most weighty trust and highest honor*" (*The Desire of Ages,* pp. 224, 225; italics supplied).

A similar trial with terminal cancer confronted another acquaintance. She knew that Christ was first and foremost in her life; so when she was afflicted with cancer she determined to trust Him no matter what. She also believed that Jesus loved her supremely and desired her best, and so she availed herself of whatever solution He had in mind for her. She reasoned that if her loving earthly father would do whatever it took to help her, then how much more her loving heavenly Father. For reasons God alone knows, He chose to miraculously heal her of all cancer.

We may not understand God's answers in situations like these, but we are sure that whatever He does, as we avail ourselves of His will, is for our best. God knows exactly what He is doing. And He is in the perfect position to know, for He sees the beginning from the end, the total spectrum.

SOLDIERS IN THE LORD'S ARMY

A dying young man once told his father that he was a faithful soldier in the Lord's army. The war of the great controversy was raging on, and as in every war good soldiers get hurt. Some survive, but some do get wounded, maimed, even killed. But in both sickness and health they are upheld by His loving, nail-scarred hands. In both life and death they are embraced by His love. Nothing ever can separate us from the love of God. We are good soldiers in His army, and through everything we must remain resolute and faithful. Hope and confidence fill our hearts because we know that ultimately the war is won in our favor. And some day soon the tombs of God's fallen warriors will be torn asunder, and together we will rejoice forever in God's glorious victory.

"Therefore we do not lose heart. Even though our outward man is perishing, yet the inward man is being renewed day by day. For our light affliction, which is but for a moment, is working for us a far more exceeding and eternal weight of glory, while we do not look at the things which are seen, but at the things which are not seen. For the things which are seen are temporary, but the things which are not seen are eternal" (2 Cor. 4:16–18).

QUESTIONS FOR DISCUSSION

1. What difference does focusing on the Son of man make in our prayer life? Explain why.

2. Compare and contrast some characteristics of a "pillow prayer" and a "pillar prayer." What kind of praying do you find yourself engaged in? What difference does this make?

3. The ladder is anchored in both heaven and earth. How do you relate this to the human and divine arms of Jesus that embrace you as we pray? How can this affect your prayers?

4. What do you see when you pray: a pathway or a veil? Why is it so crucial to cling to and climb upon Jesus when we pray? How does He become the medium of our prayers?

5. Why is it so important to be embraced by Christ's love when we pray? Explain the involvement and cooperation of Gabriel and Michael in answering our prayers.

6. Through the blood of Christ we have free and complete access into God's presence. Explain how this affects your attitude in prayer. What does it mean to be clothed in Christ's priestly vestments as we enter into His intercessions?

7. How does the realization that you are a combatant in the Lord's army help you endure suffering? Sharing in Christ's suffering bestows upon us the greatest honor. Share a personal experience in which this reality became evident in your life.

CHAPTER SEVEN

Praying in the Spirit

"Likewise the Spirit also helps in our weaknesses.
For we do not know what we should pray for as we ought,
but the Spirit Himself makes intercession for us with
groanings which cannot be uttered" (Romans 8:26).

Once I sent bulletin information to be used at a church where I was scheduled to preach. I had entitled the sermon "How to Prepare for the Spirit's Second Advent." But upon arriving there Sabbath morning, I noticed that the sermon title was modified to "How to Prepare for Christ's Second Advent." Whoever changed the title was no doubt trying to help the preacher out, assuming that I inadvertently made a mistake. This did not take me completely by surprise, and reinforced my observation that we seem to be more comfortable with Christ than with the Spirit. Of course, the new title did not reflect at all what I was attempting to convey in my message. The sermon was about the Holy Spirit being poured out the *second time* in the form of the latter rain, just prior to Christ's second advent.

UNCOMFORTABLE WITH THE COMFORTER?

I wonder why sometimes we are not comfortable with the Holy Spirit, the one described as the Comforter. Why we do not seek His help, especially when He is called our helper? In times of need we gravitate toward people who possess the spiritual gifts of comforting and helpfulness. So why are we not drawn to the Holy Spirit, whose very essence and function is to comfort and help us? I believe it is because we do not think that the Spirit is as close to us as Christ is. Yet there is an intimate relationship between Christ and the Spirit, and when we are close to one we are indeed close to the other. This is quite evident from what Jesus says to His disciples in John 14. Both the Spirit and Christ dwell in us (verses 17, 20), and likewise both the Father and the Son make their abode in us (verse 23). In a glorious and mysterious way all the three persons of the tri-une God dwell in us and manifest themselves through us. All three are united harmoniously in their work for us.

The same Greek word, *parakletos* in verses 16 and 26 of John 14, is used interchangeably to describe the second and third persons of the Godhead. The Spirit is all what Jesus is to us. He embraces us with His love and intercession like Jesus does. What an awesome gift Christ gave us in giving us the Spirit! He is the answer to Christ's prayer. "And I will pray the Father," He said to His disciples, "and He will give you another Helper, that He may abide with you forever" (John 14:16). God always answers the prayer of His Son, and if we are willing, He will assuredly fill us with the ever-abiding Spirit. There He helps us in our prayers as He prays for us and with us. He is well qualified to do so because He knows the mind of God and prays according to the will of God (Rom. 8:27). Like Christ, He helps in our prayer life by interceding passionately for us with intense groaning.

HIS GROANINGS EMBRACE OUR GROANINGS
There are three references to *groaning* in Romans 8.

The first reference depicts the entire creation groaning. "For we know that the whole creation groans and labors with birth pangs together until now" (verse 22). Here Paul aptly likens the groaning of God's creation to a woman in travail, struggling to deliver her child. It is clear that our world is in birth pangs, weighed down with intense pain. Pollution, crime, disease, violence, terrorism, and war are rampant. The whole creation cries out for relief and deliverance from its plight.

The second reference to groaning in Romans 8 is to God's people who groan to be delivered at the coming of Christ. "Not only that, but we also who have the firstfruits of the Spirit, even we ourselves groan within ourselves, eagerly waiting for . . . the redemption of our body" (verse 23). We groan within ourselves when we see evil at work. We groan when we battle temptations and struggle with trials. And we cry out, "When, O Lord, will You deliver us from this body of sin! O Lord hasten that day of deliverance!"

The third reference to groaning in Romans 8, however, has to do with the Holy Spirit fervently interceding for us. "Likewise the Spirit also helps in our weaknesses. For we do not know what we should pray for as we ought, but the Spirit Himself makes intercession for us with groanings which cannot be uttered" (verse 26). This third reference begins with the word "likewise," to indicate that the Holy Spirit steps into the fray and swallows up our human groanings in His divine groanings. Therefore we never need to groan alone when we pray, for the great Comforter is always at our side, absorbing our groanings in His.

Do you recall a time when you heard someone groan

in distress? I will never forget the sound of agonized groaning coming from a man injured in an auto accident and trapped behind his steering wheel. His ribs were crushed, and blood was oozing out of his mouth. His tortured groanings were gut-wrenching as he struggled between life and death. It was obvious that every fiber of his being was in tremendous travail and agony.

Let us shift the attention from this man's groaning to the divine and mighty groanings of the Holy Spirit. If that injured man's groaning gripped me to the core, then imagine the awesome groanings of the Spirit. They must reverberate across the universe with utmost passion and power. And if we inquire of Him, "For whom are You groaning and interceding?" He would readily respond, "It is all for you!"

What a gripping thought to ponder! His groaning is not only all-powerful but all-wise and all-compassionate, and we are included in this power, wisdom, and compassion. According to Romans 8:26 and 27, we are weak and finite in our praying, for we do not know what to pray for or how to pray. But God steps in to search our hearts and to know the intents of our souls. He does this for us while He fully knows the mind of the Spirit. In turn, "the Spirit searches all things, yes, the deep things of God" (1 Cor. 2:10). Hence God takes our heartfelt but finite prayers and lines them up with the infinite mind of the Spirit.

Then the passionate intercessions of the Spirit enfold our puny prayers and process them according to the will of God. Our prayers are indeed weak because we do not know what or how to pray as we ought. That is the "weakness" referred to in Romans 8:26—the weakness of our prayers for which the Spirit comes to our aid. Notice the immediate and close correlation between such weakness and our deficient prayers. The identification of one with the other is apparent. Thus the Holy Spirit comes to help us precisely where we need help.

PRAYING IN THE SPIRIT

Now let us go further in understanding what it means to pray in the Spirit. The apostle Paul presents this idea in Ephesians 6:18. He admonishes the believers: "Praying always with all prayer and supplication in the Spirit, being watchful to this end with all perseverance and supplication for all the saints." According to the three texts we have mentioned (Rom. 8:26, 27; 1 Cor. 2:10, 11; and Eph. 6:18), we are to:

1. Pray for all the saints.

2. Pray according to the will of God.

3. Pray in the Spirit.

But how do we pray in the Spirit and according to the will of God, considering that we do not know how or what to pray for as we ought? The answer comes from the above three Pauline texts.

1. The Holy Spirit helps us in our inability or "weakness" of not knowing how or what to pray for. He completely swallows up our weak groanings of intercession in His mighty groanings of intercession.

2. The Holy Spirit connects us with the divine mind of God. God knows our hearts and inner motives and He knows the mind of the Spirit; and likewise the Spirit knows the mind of God (Rom. 8:27; 1 Cor. 2:10, 11). Thus in the Spirit we are mysteriously and mutually connected to God. He searches our hearts and discerns the sin-

cere motives of our weak prayers. In turn the Holy Spirit, who knows the mind of God and our humble petitions, makes intercession for us in our weakness.

3. The Holy Spirit, the Comforter who abides with us forever, includes our weak intercessions in His mighty intercessions. "Because He [the Holy Spirit] makes intercession for the saints according to the will of God" (Rom. 8:27). This is praying in the Spirit according to the will of God.

"PASSIONATE DESIRE INTO STILL SUBMISSION"

This pertinent statement was found in Ellen White's old Bible, in her own handwriting. It reveals how our humble prayers merge into the will of God: "The prayer that does not succeed in modulating our wishes; in changing the passionate desire into still submission; the anxious tumultuous expectation into quiet surrender is not true prayer. The life is most holy in which there is least of petition and desire and most of waiting upon God, that in which petition often passes into thanksgiving. Pray till prayer makes you forget your own wishes and leaves or merges them into God's will. The divine wisdom has given us prayer, not as a means to obtain the good things of earth, but as a means whereby we learn to do without them, not as a means to escape evil, but as a means whereby we become strong to meet it."

God's all-encompassing will is revealed through His infinite love and wisdom toward us. We are acquainted with just a small part of our own reality, and even that minute acquaintance is incomplete. But God thoroughly knows the total spectrum of reality—past, present, and future. And He delights to apply such resources—His knowledge mingled with His unconditional love—to our circumstances. Wouldn't you and I want to trust Him, taking full advantage of His great love and vast resources by allowing our will to be absorbed in His? Jesus gives us such example when He prayed to His Father: "Nevertheless, not as I will, but as You will" (Matt. 26:39).

If we could see things from God's vantage point we would never want anything but His will. "God never leads His children otherwise than they would choose to be led, if they could see the end from the beginning and discern the glory of the purpose which they are fulfilling as coworkers with Him." Thus "our lives may be the simple outworking of His will. As we commit our ways to Him, He will direct our steps" (*The Ministry of Healing,* p. 479). How grateful we should be to the Holy Spirit for clothing our prayers with His intercessions. He takes the intents of the heart, notes the innermost motives of the soul, and then molds these into His groanings and in harmony with the will of God. Thus when we look back at some of our prayers, we are full of gratitude that God chose not to answer us in the way we asked. So what does is it mean to pray and supplicate "in the Spirit" (Eph. 6:18)? It is when we humbly submit our weak prayers to the inexpressible groanings of the Spirit who knows well the will of God.

GOD'S RELENTLESS SEARCH

How does considering the will of God apply to our prayer life? How does it apply to our intercessions for the needs of others? In Ezekiel 22:30 (a text alluded to in another chapter), God tells us about His relentless search for someone to stand in the gap on behalf of others. "So I sought for a man among them," God says, "who would make a wall, and stand in the gap before Me on behalf of the land, that I should not destroy it; but I found no one." It is God's earnest desire to find someone to pray for the land [the people], but unfortunately He often comes up empty-handed. This text shows us that intercessory prayer is never humanly generated but divinely inspired. The desire to intercede that seizes our hearts issues forth from the very heart of God.

God knows that praying in the Holy Spirit according to His will does make a difference. It is not a desperate attempt on our part to convince Him to act in a certain way, or to weary Him into finally changing His mind. It is not like a spoiled child finally extracting a treat or a toy from his reluctant parent. Rather, it is giving God the opportunity to accomplish His will in ways He otherwise would not have. Our humble and persevering intercessions for others, interwoven with the groanings of the Spirit according to the will of God, enable Him to move in providential ways to honor our faith.

God needs such faithful intercessors to cooperate with Him so that He may fulfill what He desires, not what we demand or deserve. Notice the subjunctive formulation of our text: "that I *should not* destroy it." In other words, there are judgments that God is completely justified to execute but that He would rather not execute. Compare this to a loving father who must mete out punishment to his rebellious child but does not like to do it. Diligently he searches to find an alternative way of dealing with the situation.

Whenever I study this text in Ezekiel I readily connect it with the story of Jonah, the reluctant prophet. God did not want to come up empty-handed in His search for someone to stand in the gap, to reach out in warning and intercession to the land of Nineveh. Do you see why God so doggedly pursued the fleeing Jonah, even to the depths of the sea? He did not want to destroy the land, the "more than one hundred and twenty thousand persons" of wicked Nineveh (Jonah 4:11). Jonah's cooperation was needed to fulfill God's desire of not destroying but rather saving the wicked inhabitants of Nineveh.

Jonah's ministry, though somewhat reluctant, was crucial in executing God's overall plan. Something did happen that would not have happened had Jonah not cooperated with God. Jonah exhorted, the people repented, and God relented. "Then God saw their works, that they turned from their evil way; and God relented from the disaster that He had said He would bring upon them, and He did not do it" (Jonah 3:10). Praise God! He is in the business of salvation, not destruction.

Interceding for others in the Spirit is carrying the burdens of the Spirit for the salvation of others. Indeed, we partake of God's travail for His lost children. Ellen White suggests a practical expression of praying in the Spirit, making us effective disciples in Christ's service. " 'Praying always with all prayer and supplication in the Spirit,' praying in the closet, in the family, in the congregation, everywhere. . . . They feel that souls are in peril, and with earnest, humble faith they plead the promises of God in their behalf. The ransom paid by Christ . . . is ever before them. They will have souls as seals of their ministry"

(*Testimonies,* vol. 5, p. 190).

DRIVEN BY THE SPIRIT

Philip the evangelist is a prime example of how the Holy Spirit comes near to us and aligns our prayers and witness with His intercessions and God's grand strategy of saving the lost (Acts 8:26-40). The treasurer of Queen Candace of Ethiopia was continuing to search for truth as he traveled back home by way of Gaza. Apparently this honest seeker for truth did not find what he was looking for in Judea. But the Holy Spirit could not bear to see him go home without the saving knowledge of the resurrected Jesus. He knew exactly the location of this traveler and the details of his journey, and so He said to Philip, "Go near and overtake this chariot" (verse 29).

And then after the eunuch was baptized, "the Spirit of the Lord caught Philip away, so that the eunuch saw him no more" (verse 39). The Holy Spirit was well acquainted with this Ethiopian traveler, and foresaw the great potential of many who would be led to Christ through his witness back in his homeland. He and Philip were both open to the leading of the Holy Spirit, and thus the right circumstances and persons miraculously synchronized in accomplishing God's grand purpose.

Likewise, as we cooperate with and pray in the Spirit, He will providentially lead us to specific locations and circumstances where we can reach specific persons for Jesus. Such experiences are serendipitous indeed. Every day becomes an adventure as you trust the Spirit's leading and anticipate how He is going to surprise you. "Jesus knows us individually, and is touched with the feeling of our infirmities. He knows us all by name. He knows the very house in which we live, the name of each occupant. He has at times given directions to His servants to go to a certain street in a certain city, to such a house, to find one of His sheep" (*The Desire of Ages,* p. 479).

THE SECOND ADVENT OF THE SPIRIT

Soon we will witness the sprinkling of the Holy Spirit swell into the mighty outpouring of the latter rain. Just as the early rain caused the gospel seed to *germinate* and grow, so the latter rain will *ripen* the harvest in these final days of earth's history. As mentioned in this chapter's introduction, the second coming of the Spirit will precede the second coming of Jesus. Just as, in converse relationship, the first coming of the Holy Spirit followed the first coming of Jesus. We cannot be ready for Christ's coming unless we are first prepared by the Spirit's coming. This is our first and foremost priority: to pray in the Spirit, to witness in the Spirit, and to hunger and thirst for the mighty outpouring of the Spirit. The promise is that miracles, signs, and wonders will accompany the faithful remnant, sweeping over the globe with the last warning message. Will you and I be a part of it?

As the disciples prayed, hungered, and thirsted for the early rain, so we are to pray, hunger, and thirst for the latter rain. Their gift of the early rain was to germinate the gospel grain, our gift of the latter rain will be to ripen the gospel harvest. The Holy Spirit descends when we truly cherish Him and earnestly seek Him. When in humility our measly prayers unite with Jesus' mighty prayers. When the Spirit's fervent groanings enfold our faint groanings.

The refreshing will come when we truly learn to pray with the Intercessor and pray in the Comforter. "The great work of the gospel is not to close with less manifestation of the power of God than marked its opening. The prophecies which were fulfilled in the outpouring of the former rain at the opening of the gospel are again to be fulfilled in the latter rain at its close" (*The Great Controversy*, pp. 611, 612).

Empowered by the outpouring of the latter rain to reap the ripening harvest, "servants of God, with their faces lighted up and shining with holy consecration, will hasten from place to place to proclaim the message from heaven. By thousands of voices, all over the earth, the warning will be given. Miracles will be wrought, the sick will be healed, and signs and wonders will follow the believers. Satan also works with lying wonders, even bringing down fire from heaven in the sight of men. Revelation 13:13. Thus the inhabitants of the earth will be brought to take their stand. The message will be carried not so much by argument as by the deep conviction of the Spirit of God" (*ibid.*, p. 612).

QUESTIONS FOR DISCUSSION

1. Why is it that some of us are not as comfortable with the Spirit as we are with Jesus? What are some thoughts that may help us to feel more comfortable with the "Comforter"?

2. Can you recall a "groaning experience" in your prayer life? How can the Spirit's fervent groanings swallow up our faint groanings?

3. How does knowing that the Spirit intercedes with

such intensity for you affect your faith? Compare the relationship between the intercessions of Jesus and those of the Spirit.

4. What does it mean for you to "pray in the Spirit"? How does it work? How does this lead you to pray according to God's will? How does it impact your witness to others?

5. When it comes to cooperation with the will of God in reaching out to the lost, with whom would you identify more, Jonah or Philip? Explain why. Remember: God used both.

6. When God comes searching for someone to stand in the gap, to intercede on behalf of others, does He find one in your church, in your home, in you? How diligently does He need to search? Does He sometimes come up empty-handed? Why?

7. What would it take to help you prepare for the second advent of the Holy Spirit? Clarify the relation between this preparation and your preparation for the second advent of Christ.

CHAPTER EIGHT

The Eyes of the Lord

"For the eyes of the Lord run to and fro throughout the whole earth, to show Himself strong on behalf of those whose heart is loyal to Him" (2 Chronicles 16:9).

PHILIP AND THE ETHIOPIAN

When we intercede for others, we must see them with the heart of Jesus. We will look at the heart and not at the outward appearance. This lesson became painfully clear to me when I landed in a major American airport. On my way to the car rental place I thought of the prayers I had offered with Jesus and in the Spirit on behalf of those God sends my way. And then when I found myself standing before the agents' counter, I edged myself away from one particular agent, hoping that someone else would help me. I confess that in this situation I was not exactly looking at the heart.

Paradoxically yet providentially, the very agent I was hoping would not help me was the very one who offered his help. The first question he asked was about insurance. I responded that my organization provided insurance for car rentals. "What organization do you represent?" he asked. I usually respond that I am a professor at such a university. But this time the Lord, who saw this agent's heart and had already prepared the way for our paths to cross, led me to say, "I am an ordained minister of the Seventh-day Adventist Church."

He seemed to be pleasantly surprised, telling me that he had been hoping and praying for several days to meet an Adventist. Becoming better acquainted, he confided that he had grown up in an Adventist home in Ethiopia. However, upon immigrating to this country as a youngster, he and his family had left God and the church. That was nearly 20 years earlier. Now he had been strongly convicted to return to God and the church. As a child, his favorite Bible story from Sabbath school was that of Philip and the Ethiopian. Remarking that my name was also Philip, he felt that I was like Philip the evangelist whom the Holy Spirit had used to reach the Ethiopian traveler. With deep conviction he stated that in God's providence a modern-day Philip the evangelist had met a modern-day Ethiopian seeker.

PRAY FOR LABORERS

Indeed the eyes of the Lord are relentlessly searching for persons and opportunities to show His strength through our witness (2 Chron. 16:9). God searches not only for the ones who need help but for the helpers as well. He diligently looks for His people to come before Him to touch other people's lives (Eze. 22:30). Jesus also conveys this concept of divine-human cooperation in saving the lost. "But when He saw the multitudes, He was moved with compassion for them, because they were weary and scattered, like sheep having no shepherd. Then He said to His disciples, 'The harvest truly is plentiful, but the laborers are few. Therefore pray the Lord of the harvest to send out laborers into His harvest'" (Matt. 9:36-38).

Looking more closely at the context of this account, we

notice that Jesus manifested a special kind of seeing—seeing with the heart. The kind of seeing that moved Him with compassion for the weary, scattered, and lost. The genius of Christ's compassion was to be bequeathed to His disciples. They were to see the weary ones with the heart and compassion of their Master. What He said about the plentiful harvest and the few laborers might have surprised them. They may have thought, as we do today, that the opposite was reality. That the harvest was meager, that the laborers were all right. This view originates from looking at the outward appearance instead of the heart. But Jesus knows the heart and He gave an accurate assessment of the situation.

HIS HEART'S DESIRE

Notice the contrast in His truthful assessment of the situation. The harvest: plentiful. The laborers: few. How does Jesus resolve this apparent paradox? What does He resort to in solving this dilemma? "Therefore," He continues, "pray the Lord of the harvest to send out laborers into His harvest." He appeals specifically to *prayer*. In His love, wisdom, and providence He discerns that prayer is the answer. It is the desire of His heart to make this prayer request a reality in our lives. Answering this prayer request is indeed always according to God's will. Let's answer the desire of Jesus' heart. Let's avail ourselves as witnesses in His hands to a lost and hurting world.

As we fulfill the desire of Jesus' heart and entrust ourselves to Him as compassionate laborers, He then opens the floodgates of His providence on our behalf. Remember, His eyes "run to and fro throughout the whole earth, to show Himself strong on behalf of those whose heart is loyal to Him" (2 Chron. 16:9). As we entrust ourselves to Him every day, praying that He would use us in His harvest, He delights to manifest His strength and grace through our weakness. He is able to do "above all that we ask or think, according to the power that works in us" (Eph. 3:20). His infinite ability is translated into a power that is active within us.

This is precisely what makes serving Christ such a serendipitous experience. He pleasantly surprises us as He miraculously works out His will into our experience. He providentially brings individuals and circumstances to click together. It is exciting every day to anticipate what God has "up His sleeve" to reward our trust in Him. How can our Christian witness ever be boring? It transforms our lives into an exciting spiritual adventure. Enter into the exciting serendipity of God!

Jesus Passes by our Nazareth

The Lord is diligently searching for those who would cooperate with Him in interceding for others (Eze. 22:30). We never have to convince Him of that. It is His divine joy and will for us to pray, and it does make a difference. Such currents of goodwill and blessing are available to us. The dam is ready to be released, awaiting our trust and cooperation. Look at the mighty work Jesus intended to accomplish towards the people of Nazareth, His hometown. "Now He did not do many mighty works there," Matthew explains, "because of their unbelief" (13:58).

What a tremendous loss! Jesus came to His hometown having in mind to accomplish great miracles, but the people's lack of trust in Him blocked His plan. One wonders what and how many mighty works He might have performed if their hearts had been open to Him. For their lack of trust was apparently the only thing that kept the flow of His blessings away from them. Can we imagine this happening to us today? Regrettably, it happens all too often. The Lord passes by our own "Nazareths" to actualize the blessings which He intends for us and for others who come into our sphere of influence. Why do we hinder His blessings and let Him leave disappointed? Why not let Him work out His wonderful plan unhindered? Why not let Him show His strength in our behalf by closing tight the doors of unbelief in our hearts and opening wide the gates of faith?

Someone once said that the prevailing winds of God's opportunities are always blowing; the question is whether our sails are furled wide open to catch them. Do we sing "Fill my cup, Lord" while holding our cup upside down? A tightly sealed bottle may float forever in the vast ocean without the hope of one droplet ever penetrating it. We too are engulfed by Christ's mighty currents of grace and intercession. But do we open our hearts wide for a spiritual submersion?

A story is told of a man who went fishing in a nearby lake. He was fortunate to catch plenty of big fish that day. But to his friend's surprise, he would throw back into the water each one of the fish the moment he would reel it in. Curiously, his friend asked him why he was getting rid of all these big fish. "They are too big for my 10-inch frying pan." Are we a 10-inch-frying-pan people, like him? As "fishers of men," do we use only a 10-inch frying pan? Are we afraid to get outside our little box of limitations? Why not enlarge our capacity to receive His abundance so that we "may be filled with all the fullness of God"? Why not believe that He "is able to do exceedingly abundantly above all that we ask or think, according to the power that works in us" (Eph. 3:19, 20)?

A HANDFUL OF FLOUR AND A LITTLE OIL

Our prayers may be weak and our resources scarce, yet in God's hands they become prevailing and plentiful. Consider the story of the widow of Zarephath recorded in 1 Kings 17. This woman was a Phoenician, not even an Israelite, yet God multiplied her meager gifts when they were submitted to Him. In the deadly drought plaguing that whole region, Elijah asked her to give him the last morsel of food she possessed. Look at the bleak situation she was confronting. "I do not have bread, only a handful of flour in a bin, and a little oil in a jar," she confessed to Elijah, "and see, I am gathering a couple of sticks that I may go in and prepare it for myself and my son, that we may eat it, and die" (verse 12).

A destitute widow and her child barely surviving the drought and ensuing famine, and desperately trying to hold death at bay as long as possible. A little flour, a little oil, a couple of sticks, their last measly meal before certain death. That was her reality as she viewed it, but it was not God's reality. Here enters the prophet Elijah asking for the pittance she had. And she gave it all, trusting that God would provide. God did provide, for whatever little she had given from her hands soon became much in God's hands.

Shortly thereafter, however, her only son became terribly ill and died. Again Elijah asked for what she had—her dead son. And just as she had earlier given him her scarce provisions, now she gives her dead hope—her only son. But in God's hands hope springs forth from hopelessness, life from where there is only death. She hands over her dead son, who had "no breath left in him," and God through Elijah returns him now breathing the fullness of life.

WITH GOD ALL THINGS ARE POSSIBLE

Let's enlarge our capacity to receive His abundance: a little trickle of our prayer plunged into the mighty Niagara Falls of Jesus' prayers. A smelly and tainted prayer offered with the "much incense" of Jesus' intercessions. A pillow prayer transformed into a pillar prayer, aligning itself with Jesus, the mystical ladder, and reaching the gates of heaven. From a little flour and oil into abundant feasting, and from death unto life. "With men this is impossible," Jesus said, "but with God all things are possible" (Matt. 19:26).

"The humblest workers, in *cooperation* with Christ, may touch chords whose vibrations shall ring to the ends of the earth and make melody throughout eternal ages. Heavenly intelligences are waiting to *cooperate* with human instrumentalities, that they may reveal to the world what human beings may become, and what, through *union* with the Divine, may be accomplished for the saving of souls that are ready to perish. There is *no limit* to the usefulness of one who, putting self aside, makes room for the work of the Holy Spirit upon his heart and lives a life wholly consecrated to God. . . . The inexhaustible supplies of heaven are at their command. . . . To everyone who offers himself to the Lord for service, withholding nothing, is given power for the attainment of *measureless* results. For these God will do great things" (*The Ministry of Healing*, pp. 159, 160; italics supplied).

Let our eyes, with the Lord's, run to and fro all around us so that we may see beyond our limited reality and discern His limitless reality. Elijah was God's anointed prophet, and yet he ran for his life from Jezebel because he saw only his limited reality. Can you imagine Elijah giving even a slight thought to Jezebel and her henchmen while he was being translated into heaven? This was God's reality transcending his reality. His mortality put on immortality and was carried by a fiery chariot and a whirlwind of angelic hosts into the very presence of God.

THE UNSEEN TRANSCENDS THE SEEN

From God's perspective, what we see is less real than what we don't see. For what we see is limited and temporary, but what we don't see is limitless and eternal. This is why we must always see through our heart of faith God's glorious realm in the midst of our daily predicaments. The apostle Paul said that "we do not look at the things which are seen, but at the things which are not seen. For the things which are seen are temporary, but the things which are not seen are eternal" (2 Cor. 4:18).

Elisha learned this lesson well from his mentor Elijah. He had seen the glory of God when Elijah passed the mantle on to him. Later on, when the mighty Syrian army with its formidable horses and chariots surrounded him, he was not at all intimidated, for he already had seen God's fiery chariot and whirlwind. Now he was seeing the whole mountain ablaze with God's glory and His chariots of fire.

The worry of Elisha's servant, unfortunately, may more

aptly represent the experience of many of us today. It is quite human to be so caught up in what is "lesser seen"—the immediate crises at hand—that we become oblivious to the "greater unseen." Elisha's servant was beside himself. His vision was confined to the immediate and seemingly insurmountable obstacles. "Alas, my master!" he helplessly cried out. "What shall we do?" The prophet's focus was on what God had already done, and so he confidently answered, "Do not fear, for those who are with us are more than those who are with them" (2 Kings 6:15, 16).

Capturing the spirit of 2 Chronicles 16:9, Elisha prayed that his servant would see beyond his sight to the eyes of the Lord running to and fro throughout the whole earth (including Dothan), showing Himself strong in behalf of His trusting and loyal servants. We have modern-day Dothans on every side. God wants us to view our Dothans through His potential deliverance and not through our imaginary defeat. Looking to the God of the possible in the midst of the humanly impossible makes all the difference.

OPEN OUR EYES

From our human perspective, some formidable challenges seem to have no solutions whatsoever. We find ourselves hedged in on every side, with no possibility of disentanglement from our terrible predicament. It's like being confined in a darkened room without a door or windows, lost in impenetrable darkness. From the dark corner of our world there may seem to be no way out, but from God's perspective there is always a way of escape. From God's perspective there is no hopeless confinement or abysmal darkness. He is there to provide us with breakthroughs that we could never have even imagined. "In *every* difficulty He has His way prepared to bring relief. Our heavenly Father has a *thousand ways* to provide for us, of which we know *nothing*" (*The Desire of Ages,* p. 330; italics supplied).

Back to our story of Elisha and his servant. "And Elisha prayed, and said, 'Lord, I pray, open his eyes that he may see.' Then the Lord opened the eyes of the young man, and he saw. And behold, the mountain was full of horses and chariots of fire all around Elisha" (2 Kings 6:17). Two men looking at the same momentous crisis: one's eyes filled with God's vision; the other's filled with his own. Here, once again, the answer is *prayer!* "Lord, I *pray,* open his eyes that he may see." Those who are anchored in that position of strength and are tasting the glories of the unseen must pray for those who are not. Thus, one by one, visions of glorious unseen realities may flash among the people of God. This kind of vision is indispensable in facing the crises that confront God's remnant people in the last days. For without such vision the people perish.

Elijah and Elisha represent the faithful ones who will be translated and resurrected at the glorious coming of Christ. Like us they were often faced with obstacles that tested them to the core, but they confronted their fear with the faith that sees beyond the immediate. Such living faith is contagious. The Lord Himself mentored Elijah, who bequeathed his mantle to Elisha, and who in turn helped his servant to see a vision of God. We who live in the closing hours of earth's history need to experience such a living faith so that we can share this glorious vision with those within our sphere of influence. Without a vision we perish.

IN THE TWINKLING OF AN EYE

When we share in God's vision, He expands our horizons and shows us how He transforms our obstacles into opportunities. Recently the Lord opened my eyes to see an impossibility become a possibility. I arrived at a major U.S. airport to catch my flight, and I found the place in a pandemonium. Because of adverse weather conditions, flights were delayed or canceled, and stranded passengers were becoming frazzled. How could God's vision become my vision in reaching out to this stressed-out crowd? Was His harvest plentiful in this situation? Was He looking for willing laborers who would see beyond the outward appearance? Was He looking for praying laborers who would see with the heart of Jesus and join Him in His intercessions for others? Was He looking for me? Would I say to Him, "Here am I; send me"?

With a prayer in my heart, I felt impressed to talk to a certain woman finishing a phone call to her family. She seemed quite distressed about flying. When she finished, I struck up a friendly conversation with her. She began to tell about her anxiousness in traveling by air, but insisted that flying was a necessity since she had to attend medical conventions. Feeling more at ease with me, she began to tell me about her specialty, cosmetic surgery: "I make people look and feel better about themselves," she said. I tactfully inquired if some clients come back to see her more than once or twice. I did not have a clue as to where the Lord was leading me with this, but I believed that He was praying and reaching out with me. And I trusted the promise that the Holy Spirit would give me the right words to say at the opportune time.

To my last question she responded rather impatiently that her patients did not normally see her again and again for cosmetic procedures. Risking my luck, and taking advantage of her sense of humor, I pressed the point. "Why not?" I asked. "Because," she blurted out, "they get old, their skin gets wrinkled, and there isn't much left to work with!" "What happens then?" I persisted. "Nothing, sir, they just shrivel up and die, that's what! They simply shrivel up and die!" She wondered why I was so interested. Then she curiously looked at my face and joked: "Well, sir, you need a lot of help yourself!"

I sensed clearly that this was God's providential opening for me. Seizing the opportunity, I said in one breath: "You are absolutely right. I look terrible, Mr. Universe looks bad; Miss Universe looks ugly; even you, Doctor, with all due respect, do not look that hot compared to how the divine cosmetic surgeon Jesus will make us look like when He comes again." And without pause I continued: "The Bible says that in a twinkling of an eye He will fashion our ugly bodies after His own glorious body. He is going to make us look perfect forever, and that will be the day!" She startled me when she responded quite positively: "If what you said is really true, it will sure change my approach to my practice." She explained that her work would become more rewarding, for she would be able to give her patients more than temporary help and hope. "Could you show me the truth of what you are saying from the Bible?" she asked.

A PHYSICIAN MEETS THE GREAT PHYSICIAN

For more than an hour I shared several biblical promises about the blessed hope, and a Bible study ensued on this all-important subject. She became so absorbed in the discussion that we both forgot about our delayed flight, until an announcement reminded us to prepare for boarding. More than 300 passengers were boarding, and at the gate I had to interrupt the discussion with the surgeon so that I could take my turn. Reaching my window seat— 32A—I wished that I could have continued the interesting conversation. But I comforted myself by saying that I had planted the seed and someone else would water it. But my disappointment did not last long. A few minutes later this surgeon stood by where I was seated, exclaiming in disbelief that her seat number was 32B! I was quite surprised myself, but now certain that God was providentially leading us to carry on this important discussion about Christ and His soon coming. She sat down, and we resumed our interrupted Bible study.

As we prepared for landing, the Spirit of God seemed to be gripping her heart with conviction about the truth she was hearing, and she decided to commit her life to Christ. In God's providence this earthly physician was committing herself to the Great Physician. This human cosmetic surgeon was submitting her life to the divine Cosmetic Surgeon, who in a moment and in the twinkling of an eye will transform our lowly bodies into His glorious body. Praise God!

"For the eyes of the Lord run to and fro throughout the whole earth, to show Himself strong on behalf of those whose heart is loyal to Him" (2 Chron. 16:9). "Now to Him who is able to do exceedingly abundantly above all that we ask or think, according to the power that works in us, to Him be glory" (Eph. 3:20).

QUESTIONS FOR DISCUSSION

1. Why do you think the Lord greatly desires to show Himself strong on our behalf when we pray for and reach out to others? Can you recall a specific example of this in your life?

2. Why do we sometimes focus on the scarcity of the harvest but not on its plentitude? What does this tell us about seeing people around us from our own perspective? What does it mean to see with the heart? with the heart of Christ? What difference would this make?

3. How do we fulfill the desire of Christ's heart when we become laborers in His field?

4. In what ways does Jesus pass by our "Nazareth" today? What do you think makes us oblivious to His providential plans to accomplish great works in our lives?

5. What would you consider meager spiritual gifts or resources in your life and witness? Do you feel that your "handful of flour and little oil" is almost depleted? What can be done?

6. What is one thing in your life that you consider dead but long to see resurrected?

7. Explain: What we see with our eyes is less real than what we see with our souls.

8. Recall an experience when your eyes were opened to see the unseen. What brought this about? What difference has it made in your life?

Conclusion

When Afghanistan was liberated from the stifling Taliban rule, women broke out in joyous celebration for the simple pleasure of seeing sunlight again. For more than five years they were condemned to hide under their *burqas* (drab head-to-toe garments). To be bathed in full blasts of brilliant sunshine was no comparison to being imprisoned in the dimness of their *burqas*. These liberated Afghani women somehow managed to live in obscurity under their veils. However, they could discern through the dimness that there was a world of brightness and sunshine out there.

Eugene Peterson aptly describes our transition from this dim world to the brilliance of the next in *The Message*: "We don't yet see things clearly. We are squinting in a fog, peering through a mist. But it won't be long before the weather clears and the sun shines bright! We'll see it all then, see it all as clearly as God sees us, knowing him directly just as he knows us!" (1 Cor. 13:12). Peterson's rendering of this text in contemporary language gets to the heart of what Paul is trying to say. The text refers to seeing dimly in a mirror.

Today one wonders why an image in a mirror would have to be blurry. The word for "mirror" as used here in Greek, *esoptron,* refers to a piece of polished metal in ancient times. Then, one could not get a clear image, only a hazy one at best. This illustrates to us that our best spiritual knowledge and experience is only dim and diminished compared to what we will have in heaven. Yet this imperfect knowledge is sufficient as a foretaste or firstfruit of seeing Jesus, our bright Sun of Righteousness, face to face on that glorious day.

Singing the moving congregation hymn "It Is Well With My Soul" one Sabbath, I was struck with the words of the last stanza. "And Lord, haste the day when *my faith shall be sight,* the clouds be rolled back as a scroll." What an awesome thought! Someday soon, when Jesus appears in the eastern sky, we will never see dimly anymore, for we shall behold Him face to face. The faith so exercised in our prayers and our witness shall break forth into sight. When this corruptible puts on the incorruptible, there will never again be a veil obscuring our vision from the Divine. We will know Him directly as He knows us directly, advancing from glory to glory in the undimmed brightness of His glory.

Our loving God has gradually unfolded His knowledge and unveiled His glory to us. Mercifully it has been gradual, as much as we can bear without it consuming us. Now with joyous anticipation we await His ultimate unveiling when we shall see Him and be like Him. "Beloved, now we are children of God; and it has not yet been revealed what we shall be, but we know that when He is revealed, we shall be like Him, for we shall see Him as He is"

(1 John 3:2). There shall be no more sin or Satan, no more trials or temptations, no more disease or death. For "the former things have passed away" (Rev. 21:4).

The skeptical mind says that seeing is believing, but the believer in Christ testifies that believing is seeing. In this fallen world that is the best that we can hope for. Indeed, we have tasted of the world to come and we can discern even through the veil and the haze God's glorious reality. But when Christ comes again, faith shall actually become sight. No more falling and forgiveness, no more prayer of confession or cry of condemnation, no more petition or intercession, only the basking in the unveiled glory of the Lord! May the comforting rays of such glory continue to permeate our daily lives and grow ever brighter until He comes. May the embrace of our praying Jesus enfold us now until we become overwhelmed in His dazzling glory. Praise the Lord, soon we shall behold the King in His glory!

BIBLIOGRAPHY

Nichol, Francis D., ed. *The Seventh-day Adventist Bible Commentary*. Washington, D.C.: Review and Herald Pub. Assn., 1980. Vols. 6, 7.

White, Ellen G. *Christ Triumphant*. Hagerstown, Md.: Review and Herald Pub. Assn., 1999.

————. *The Desire of Ages*. Mountain View, Calif.: Pacific Press Pub. Assn., 1940.

————. *Early Writings*. Washington, D.C.: Review and Herald Pub. Assn., 1882.

————. *Education*. Mountain View, Calif.: Pacific Press Pub. Assn., 1952.

————. *Gospel Workers*. Washington, D.C.: Review and Herald Pub. Assn., 1948.

————. *The Great Controversy*. Mountain View, Calif.: Pacific Press Pub. Assn., 1950.

————. *The Ministry of Healing*. Mountain View, Calif.: Pacific Press Pub. Assn., 1948.

————. *Prophets and Kings*. Mountain View, Calif.: Pacific Press Pub. Assn., 1917.

————. *Selected Messages*. Washington, D.C.: Review and Herald Pub. Assn., 1958.

————. *Steps to Christ*. Washington, D.C.: Review and Herald Pub. Assn., 1908.

————. *Temperance*. Mountain View, Calif.: Pacific Press Pub. Assn., 1949.

————. *Testimonies for the Church*. Mountain View, Calif.: Pacific Press Pub. Assn., 1948.

————. *Thoughts From the Mount of Blessing*. Mountain View, Calif.: Pacific Press Pub. Assn., 1956.